CUBAN PALM TREES
IN MANHATTAN

CUBAN PALM TREES IN MANHATTAN

Abandoned by her husband,
a Cuban society woman
finds herself with little money
and several daughters to marry off.
Her family's reputation in tatters,
she leaves her beloved island
to begin life anew in a small
apartment in Upper Manhattan.

RON TORRES

Picture credits:
Page 144, Peraza Family Crest,
Gustavo Flores Yzaguirre, Heraldica, Pinterest.com.
Page 150, painting of Beatriz de Bobadilla y Ossorio,
Atlasunivers/Wikimedia Commons.
All other images are courtesy of the author and his relatives.

ISBN: 978-0-692-91844-9
Library of Congress Control Number: to come
Printed in the United States of America

Book design by Victoria Hartman

This book is available from www.amazon.com
or may be ordered from rontorrescreates.com.

*To the memory of
my grandmother and mother*

Contents

Author's Note

In 1986 I went to see my friend Marcia Lewis at the opening of the Broadway show *Rags*, a sequel to *Fiddler on the Roof*. The show was about Russian emigrants starting over and assimilating into New York City's culture. While I was watching the show, I couldn't help but draw comparisons to my grandmother's journey from Cuba to New York City. Right then and there, I said to myself, someday I'm going to tell her story. That idea never left my mind. I wrote little ideas here and there. After many years I got the courage to join a writing group at the Screen Actors Guild. The group was led by a very accomplished writer, Mark Weston. At these meetings everyone read aloud a chapter from their most recent writings. When my turn came, with hesitation, I read aloud my first chapter from *Cuban Palm Trees in Manhattan*. Mark said I should continue and read the next chapter as well. While I was reading it, he stopped me and asked the group, "I'm really enjoying hearing about people I know very little about. Do you want him to continue reading?" Everyone said yes. Mark encouraged me to finished this book. I will for be forever grateful to him. In the group was a newly retired English teacher, Barbara Litt. She did the first edit. Thank you, Barbara. My friend Luis Santeiro, a professional writer, also contributed to my book. Thank you, Luis. I also want to thank my copy editor, Vittorio Maestro, and book designer, Victoria Hartman, for their professional work, and my friend of forty years Paul Greco for restoring all the photographs. Last but not least is my dearest friend, Iris Labron. She and I read the entire book aloud, making changes along the way. Thank you, Iris for your untiring support.

Preface

"*No había remedio*—there was no other option. We had no choice but to leave Cuba," said Mamá, who was my maternal grandmother, Alicia Peraza. Although she was my grandmother (*abuela*), I and all of her grandchildren affectionately called her Mamá.

I'm the youngest son of Irma, Alicia's youngest daughter. I spent many afternoons listening to my grandmother tell stories of the Cuba she left behind. These stories are vignettes that danced in my mind and begged to come out. I fell in love with a place and a time I could only imagine. I loved and admired Mamá for her talents, and the quiet, dignified strength that came from her life experiences. Mamá always made me feel special. I really loved the attention she gave me, and I never tired of her Cuban stories.

Mamá was born on December 1, 1884, during Cuba's struggle for independence from Spain. Her early days were filled with the tension of the pending and inevitable war. Finally, in 1898, the Spanish-American War ended; and in 1901, after four hundred years of colonization, Cuba was free from Spain. This was a glorious time for Mamá and everyone in Cuba. Euphoria and hope filled the streets with integrated conga lines of the rich, the poor, the black and the white. A bright future was promised to everyone. This was the realization of Cuba Libre—Free Cuba.

Mamá's father, Florencio Peraza, a sugar-plantation owner, along with his first cousin, General Peraza, contributed greatly to the success of the war; and prospered handsomely as a result. Mamá, then seventeen, was the oldest daughter of ten children in the prominent Peraza family. Although she was not the most beautiful of the girls, Mamá had a lot of good qualities, and was wooed by all the young and eligible bachelors from the best Catholic families in the province because of her family's status. Without the fear of war looming over Cuba, Alicia anticipated enjoying life and the prospect of holy matrimony. But destiny had a different plan for my grandmother.

Recently, in 2014, I went to my cousin Magaly's seventy-fifth birthday. She is the oldest living Cuban family member. I told her that I was writing Mamá's story. Magaly replied, "When I first came from Cuba, a teenager at the time, I was reading some tabloid magazines. Mamá turned to me and said, 'Stop wasting your time reading that trash, and write our family story. You'll have plenty to write about.'"

When Magaly told me this, I felt a rush throughout my body, as if Mamá was sending me a direct message to write our family story. I believe Mamá sensed that I would be the scribe of her stories, our family's story. She imparted her stories intuitively, suspecting I would pass them on not only to my family, but to other Cuban immigrants, immigrants from other nations, and most of all, to women with families who are left alone to fend for themselves and their families. Everything I've written is based on Mamá and my mother's stories as they told them to me.

Mamá lived her final years not in the splendor of her free Cuba, but in a modest apartment in upper Manhattan, and because of Fidel Castro's travel restrictions, she was prohibited from ever returning to her beloved Cuba.

This is her story.

CUBAN PALM TREES
IN MANHATTAN

1

Pictures on the Wall

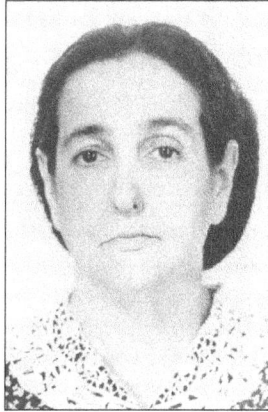

My grandmother
(Mamá), María Alicia
de la Caridad Lima
Peraza de Gongora

Summer was here, and school was out. I couldn't wait to show Mamá my report card. I knew Mamá would reward me with a dollar for getting promoted, and to a ten-year-old child in 1962, a dollar meant a lot. Visiting my grandmother was my kind of fun and filled my days. Mamá lived at the northern tip of Manhattan, at Nagle Avenue in the Inwood neighborhood. I lived at 523 West 187th Street in Washington Heights, right across the street from the Yeshiva University High School for Boys.

Getting to Mamá's house was always a fun adventure. To get there, I had to walk down what locals called Snake Hill. Properly named Fort George Hill, this was a roughly seven-block-long, steep sinuous street without any intersections that I could follow downhill from 193rd Street to Dyckman Street and Nagle Avenue, landing right on my grandmother's block. The El number 1 train would run right by her window, shaking the whole apartment. You could see the faces of the people on the passing train. Whenever a train rattled by, we had to wait to continue talking in order to be heard. We always sat in her living room as I listened to Mamá tell stories of Cuba.

Because Mamá was a teacher back in Cuba, she was someone I wanted to listen to and learn from. Whenever she spoke, I listened ever so closely because I knew Mamá was saying something important. Because I listened more than any of her other grandchildren, Mamá spent a lot of time just telling me our family's history.

Mamá lived in apartment 3A, up three long flights of stairs. I would run up the stairs really fast, and be completely out of breath by the time I reached her door. I always rang the bell really long to make sure Mamá heard me. I would hear her slow steps coming down the hall as she approached the door. Her steps had a rhythm: step, thump, step. She walked with a cane due to a broken hip from a previous fall.

"*Quién es?*" Mamá would yell.

"*Soy yo*, Ronnie."

"*Si mijo*," she would say, as she opened the door (*mijo* is an affectionate term for "my son").

I would give her a kiss on her cheek and follow her into the kitchen. I loved the way her kitchen smelled. A wonderful aroma, a combination of Cuban black coffee and ripening plantains permeated the air. Mamá would go right to the refrigerator, roll a piece of ham and Munster cheese together, and hand it to me like a prize. Even today, my favorite snack is a rolled piece of ham and Munster cheese. Mamá always looked old to me, like an old-fashioned grandmother, like the ones you'd see in black-and-white movies. She had jet-black hair, with the exception of a couple of gray hairs. People assumed she dyed her hair, but Mamá and my mother had naturally black hair well into their eighties. Mamá had a very regimented morning schedule, she rose every day at 6 A M., showered, and powdered herself. She smelled like a soft bouquet of lilacs. Whenever I visited, she was always fully dressed in a long mid-calf dress with tiny little flowers and a white embroidered collar. I didn't see my mother or any other grandmothers dressed like that. The ladies in the building where I grew up wore schmattes, or house dresses. Mamá always dressed like she expected guests. I was her most frequent guest. We were a match made in heaven. Mamá often teased my mother and said that she was no longer her youngest child; I was now her youngest. My mother would pretend to get jealous, but really loving that Mamá loved me so much.

Throughout her house were things Mamá had handcrafted. One of my favorite pieces she made was her wooden spice rack. The back panel was carved into roses and painted bright red. Mamá made a curtain with little red strawberries that wrapped around the kitchen sink to cover the plumbing. And boy, could she bake! My favorite dessert was her Buñuelos. They were like doughnuts without the hole in the middle, and covered with maple cinnamon syrup—yummy! She also baked cookies with guava in the middle. Wow!

After my snack, we would go down the hall toward the living room. In the hall was a red vinyl telephone seat that had a table attached to it, on which sat a black rotary telephone. The number was LO 9-6986. LO stood for Lorraine. In those days, there were no area codes, and every phone number started with two letters. On the walls were old photos of people I never met, but I knew they were relatives from Cuba, and I always wondered who they were.

I'd follow Mamá into the living room and sit on the couch next to her, ready to listen to her stories about Cuba. She sat at the end of her couch near her radio, resting her chin on her hand. The linoleum floor under her feet was worn from her feet shuffling back and forth. The glasses that sat slightly down on the bridge of her nose could not hide her profound sadness. I knew she was sad. I also knew my visits lifted her spirits; I always sat right next to her anticipating her stories about Cuba.

Mamá loved her long-gone world, her Cuba Libre. All she had left of that time were her memories, and talking about them was the oxygen that kept her alive. We always spoke in Spanish, even though Mamá understood and could speak some English. I only spoke Spanish with her, if you could call it that. At my home mostly English was spoken. My mother would sometimes speak to us in Spanish but we would answer her back in English. I don't remember my father speaking Spanish to me ever. Sometimes my parents spoke Spanish between them, but the only time Spanish was spoken exclusively in our house was when Mamá and my aunts would visit.

I asked Mamá, "When did you become a teacher?"

Mamá responded, "I became a teacher when I was twenty years old. Back then it was different to become a teacher. Being a teacher was the highest position a woman could aspire to, unlike the men. For example, my brothers all went to university here in the United States because the American schools had better curricula and professors. I had to go to school for two years after *la escuela principal*, then take this very long test that included every subject. Lastly, you had to go in front of a panel and answer many questions verbally."

As a schoolteacher she knew the importance of education and learning Spanish correctly. Mamá always corrected my Spanish and taught me the correct pronunciation, because she knew it would be advantageous to my future. In my early twenties I finally became proficient at speaking, reading, and writing Spanish and it has come in very handy throughout my life.

Before she could begin telling me a story, I showed her my report card. Mamá said, "*Felicidades mijo, venga conmigo*—congratulations my son, come with me.

I followed Mamá into her bedroom. Her room smelled like a drug store, a combination of Agua de Violeta and Bengay, which was pretty awful. Agua de Violeta is violet water that keeps evil spirits away. Every Cuban mother pours Agua de Violeta on her baby's head until they're grown up. I guess she used it on herself just in case. It can't hurt.

Mamá went to her nightstand, opened the drawer, and took out her keys. She went to her armoire, which was twice as tall as me and very mysterious. Mamá put the key in the door and unlocked it. She then took out a box she'd covered in a flowery fabric. She put the box on the bed, opened it, moisten her finger, and shuffled out a crisp dollar from an envelope.

"This is for you, *mijo*," Mamá said.

I kissed her and said. "*Gracias, Mamá.*"

We went back into her living room, and we took our usual places on her couch. A Cuban adventure was about to begin.

2

Cuba Libre

The Peraza family in 1894: My great-grandparents Cerila and Florencio pose with their children. Rosa stands at the far left with Clara Lisa in front of her. My grandmother is seated to the right, surrounded by her little brothers, Mario, Domingo, and Victor.

In the apartment there was this very old photograph of a family that intrigued me the most. I asked Mamá, "can I ask you about one of the pictures in the hall?" She said "Of course, *mijo*."

I went to the hall and took down the picture hanging over the red vinyl telephone seat and brought it to Mamá. "Mamá, who are these people?" I asked.

She pointed and said, "That's my father, Florencio, when he was a young man. And that's my dear mother."

"What was her name?"

"Cerila Lima. She came from a fine Portuguese family. I loved my mother so much. I still miss her. God took her so young."

"How did she die?"

"Not today, *mijo*. Someday, I'll tell you."

"Okay, Mamá." I was a persistent and curious kid. I wanted to know about my great-grandmother. She looked so elegant in the picture. So I continued, "What was your mother like?"

"She was very loving, but was also very strict. It was her job to make sure we were properly socially educated. Her family was also in the sug-arcane business, and my parents' similar backgrounds led to their ar-ranged marriage. In those days, marriages were arranged by the parents."

"You mean they had no choice in deciding who they married? What if they didn't like the way the person looked? Did they still have to marry?" I asked.

"That depended on the family."

"I wouldn't like that."

"But luckily, my parents fell madly in love."

Phew! *That's a relief*, I thought to myself.

"My parents started a family right away, and had ten children in all. I was their oldest." She pointed at this pretty, sweet-looking girl in the picture. "That's me when I was ten years old."

Trying to figure out how old my grandmother was, I asked, "What year was that picture taken?"

"It must have been in 1894, since I was born in 1884." 1884! I quickly did the math and realized Mamá was really old. She was sev-enty-eight years old!

As she pointed to a little girl in the picture, she said "That's my sis-ter Rosa, and that's my little sister Clara Lisa. We called her Catita. And those are my cute and annoying little brothers, Mario, Domingo, and Victor."

I think this is my favorite picture. My great-grandfather is standing behind my great-grandmother, and all the children surrounding them are all dressed in their very best clothes. You could tell from the pic-ture they were well off. "How rich were you?" I asked.

"My family never talked about money, but I can tell you we were well-positioned. One of things I enjoyed the most growing up were the balls."

"You mean big fancy parties with people all dressed up and danc-ing? Like in the movies?"

"Yes. But it was also a very dangerous time in Cuba."

"Why, Mamá?"

"We lived in fear because we knew war was inevitable. I knew that at some point during every party, all the men would gather in the library. Out would come my father's finest rum and cigars. My uncle, General Peraza, would start the discourse. Their voices would get louder and louder, with each man's opinion about how to beat the Spaniards. I knew the only way for Cuba to win its independence would be through war.

"You see, Cuba had been under Spanish rule since Columbus discovered it in 1492. The Cuban business owners, like my father, were tired of paying high taxes to the Spaniards, and they were only allowed to do business with them. We wanted to be free. Hence, the phrase *Cuba Libre*, which is the name of the famous drink still ordered today: rum and Coca-Cola with a squeeze of lime.

"But today, the drink is called La Mentirita—The Little Lie—because Cuba is no longer free. That assassin Fidel Castro took away everything—every freedom we fought for."

"How is it possible that a man so mean can be the president of Cuba?" I asked Mamá.

"He's not a president; he's a dictator. If you don't obey him, he kills you. At first, we all supported him. He spoke about helping the poor, educating everyone and granting equal rights for all. These promises sounded really good at the time. To make matters worse, President Kennedy failed us too, because he approved the American invasion at the Bay of Pigs but did not follow through. Many Cubans died as a result, and Cubans will never forgive Kennedy for this atrocity. Today, most Cubans who live in America vote Republican because Kennedy was a Democrat. Because of Castro, I'm still not allowed to return to Cuba to see my family, and your aunt Silvia and uncle Pancho aren't allowed to visit us either. Before Castro, Batista was our president. Everyone knew Batista was corrupt and pocketing Cuba's money. When Castro won the revolution in 1959, Batista fled to the United States in his private plane filled with Cuba's money. Yes, Batista was a thief, but at least under his rule, there was freedom."

It saddened me to hear my grandmother so filled with regret over Cuban politics.

My conversation with Mamá about Cuban politics stayed with me when, years later, I went to my friend René's party in Manhattan and met Batista's son Jorge. He was rich. His mother, the ex-First Lady of Cuba, lived in a mansion in Palm Beach, Florida. She was so rich that she would fly my friend René, who owned the beauty salon at The Pierre Hotel in New York, to Palm Beach just for the day to do her hair. The Batistas were wealthy and living high on the hog from the money they stole from Cuba, whereas the Cubans who came to the United States after Castro came into power worked hard for their success.

My friend René personifies the American Dream. He and his younger brother left Cuba in 1960 for the United States through Operation Peter Pan, a program funded by the Catholic Church. Young children were sent ahead without their parents to different parts of the United States to avoid Castro's rumored plan to send minors to the Soviet Union to serve in work camps. I can only imagine the panic these families felt.

Mamá continued, "It's been five years since I visited my country. I still can't believe I can't go home. Not even to visit my children and my grandchildren."

"Mamá, then why did you and our family come to the United States? You loved Cuba, and it was still free when you came."

Mamá responded, "I never dreamt I would ever leave my Cuba. I had to leave. I had no choice. Cuban society is very unforgiving. Your grandfather and I separated, two of my daughters tarnished our reputation, and my money was almost gone. We were ruined. I wanted a future for my four youngest daughters—Elba, Lila, Ana María, and your mother, Irma."

I ran to get her a handkerchief as tears rolled down her face. "Don't worry, Mamá. You'll be able to go back to Cuba someday. You'll see."

Mamá was quiet for a bit when she said to me, "Do you see that man in the picture?"

"Do you mean the skinny man with a big black mustache? Is he a relative, too?"

Mamá chuckled. "No, that's José Martí. He is our Cuban national hero. In 1892, he founded the Cuban Revolutionary Party. In1895, when I was eleven years old, Martí led the War of Independence. Besides his passion to free Cuba, José Martí had many other talents. He was a poet and a writer. One of his most famous works was *Versos Sencillos*, which was later adapted as the song *Guantanamera*. You know it?" Mamá started singing: "*Guantanamera, guajira Guantanamera.*"

"Yes, I do." I began singing with her.

When we finished, Mamá continued talking. "It was a dangerous time in Cuba. I remember I was afraid they were going to kill my father because he and many other sugar-plantation owners stopped producing sugar in order to hurt the Spaniards. If the Spanish government realized this, they would have hanged my father, my uncle, and all the other men who were against them."

"Did you see any fighting?

"No, most of the fighting took place in the eastern part of Cuba, in Santiago. Did you ever hear of San Juan Hill?"

"No. Tell me about it."

"The United States sent a ship to Havana called the *Maine*. No one knows for sure who or how it blew up. But the Spaniards were blamed. This was an invitation for the United States to go to war with Spain. Teddy Roosevelt and his Rough Riders marched up San Juan Hill and defeated the Spaniards. In 1898 Spain and the United States signed the Treaty of Paris, which ended the Spanish-American War. In the treaty, Spain relinquished all claim of sovereignty over Cuba. Finally, after four hundred years, Cuba was a free nation."

"You must have been so happy," I said.

"Yes, it was such a relief when the war was over. Everyone was overjoyed. We could now relax and plan our future. My younger sister Rosa was turning fifteen," she said, showing me a picture of a beautiful woman. "This is Rosa. It was the perfect time to celebrate. We began to prepare Rosa's *quinces*."

3

A Butterfly in the Sky

Mamá's sister Rosa

The *quinces*, or *fiesta de quince años*, is a debutante ball for a Catholic girl who is celebrating her fifteenth birthday. In Cuban aristocratic circles, this is also when a young lady is presented to society, including, of course, the eligible bachelors. Even today, Cubans continue this tradition in the United States. When I was a teenager, I was asked to escort young ladies celebrating their quinces because I was a good dancer. These parties are bigger than most weddings. The preparations begin several years ahead.

The girl whose quinces it is chooses her partner, usually her boyfriend or the boy she likes. She also chooses fourteen boys and fourteen girls to complete fifteen couples in total. For months, all fifteen couples rehearse the intricately choreographed dances, each of which is performed with group coordination. Always included are the waltz and the *danzón* (a dance derived from the Spanish contradanza, and with roots in English and French "figure" dancing).

Mamá began to tell me about all about Rosa's quinces. "My sweet sister Rosa could not wait to turn fifteen. She was so beautiful. Her name fit her perfectly. Every man in our town was in love with my sister."

"She looks like a movie star. Was she a movie star?"

"No, she wasn't, but she was as pretty as one. Rosa's skin was white as porcelain. She looked like a Madonna. She wore the latest European fashions, and the hairstyles that were popular at that time. Not only was she beautiful, but her talents in poetry and sculpture were magnificent.

"I will never forget the night of Rosa's quinces. My father, with Rosa on his arm, stood at the doorway waiting to be presented. It was like watching a real-life fairy tale. The announcer said, '*Señores y señoras, el distinguido Florencio Francisco Peraza, y su hija, Rosa Isabel Peraza.*' They elegantly paced into *la sala*—the ballroom—while the orchestra played the Cuban national anthem. Tears of joy flowed down everyone's face.

"Rosa was dressed in a beautiful white dress that was handmade with lace imported from Spain. Around her neck was a diamond pendant that was cut brilliantly and sparkled throughout the room. My father was dressed proudly in a beautiful navy-blue suit that was tailored just for the occasion. For the first time in many years, I saw happiness in my father's eyes.

"The tables had beautiful bouquets of roses and gardenias that perfumed the air. The servants kept bringing trays of our most delicious traditional Cuban food: suckling pigs with their heads on."

"Pigs with their heads on? Yuck!" I said.

"There were also platters of *congrí* (a combination of white rice and black beans), fried plantains, and *yuca con mojo*—cassava with garlic sauce…. The Baccarat crystal wine goblets were continually refilled with the finest French wine. I spent two days preparing all kinds of desserts, including French pastries, that I learned to bake from a servant who had lived in Paris."

"That's what we eat on Nochebuena—Christmas Eve," I said.

"Yes, and that is what Cubans eat on most special occasions. I know you love to dance. You would have loved the ten-piece orchestra that played waltzes and *danzónes* all night. My mother arranged Rosa's first dance with the wealthiest and most eligible bachelor, Julio Zell. He was second-generation German and very handsome. I was happy for my sister, but I was very disappointed."

"Why?

"I never told this to anyone, please don't repeat it."

"I swear I won't tell a soul."

"I was disappointed because I was in love with Julio, but no one knew. Since I was the oldest, I expected my mother to arrange my marriage with him. But instead, my mother chose him to be Rosa's partner for her quinces, and just like in the movies, they fell in love and were married soon after. From then on, I loved him only as a brother. My sister Rosa and both of our families were very happy, and that was the important thing."

"Where is Rosa now? Is she back in Cuba?"

"Oh, my dear sister died many years ago."

"How did she die?"

"I can't speak of this right now. It makes me too sad."

"Okay, Mamá. I guess I should be getting back home before it gets dark."

"Yes, *mijo*. Thank you for coming to see me."

"Oh, thank you for the peso, Mamá. I'll be back soon." I kissed her goodbye. While I realized it was too painful for my grandmother to speak about her sister's death, I still wanted to know.

As soon as I got home, I asked my mother, "What happened to Mamá's sister Rosa? How did she die? She was so beautiful."

My mother said, "Yes, she was, but she had a very sad ending."

"What happened?" I asked.

"Rosa married Julio in 1902, and she was very happily married for many years. But then she met Javier Macanudo. Javier was a very handsome man who was ten years younger than Rosa, and heir to the Macanudo tobacco fortune. Javier fell madly in love with Rosa, and made it known to her. She, too, had fallen in love with him; but she also knew that being a Catholic mother of five beautiful children, whom she adored, she would never abandon her husband and family.

"But how did she die?" I asked.

My mother took a long breath, and her eyes grew sad. "Mamá was in her class teaching when someone came to get her and told her that her beloved sister Rosa was dead. Nothing could have prepared Mamá for this shock. Mamá was told that Rosa had filled her bathtub with kerosene, climbed in, and lit a match, setting herself on fire. This is all anyone knows. It was such a tragedy that neither Mamá nor anyone else ever speaks of Rosa's death."

This story broke my heart. I imagine Rosa must have had some kind of a breakdown because she felt her situation had no solution. Now I understand why Mamá didn't want to talk about Rosa's death. How Mamá must have felt, losing her sister so suddenly and in such a horrifying way!

My mother, at ten years old, dealt with her grief by writing a poem about Mamá and her Tía Rosa:

Una mañana temprana en el jardin me encontraba
Junta a mi madre querida que un ramillete de rosas con su tijeras
    cortaba
Yo le pregunto asombrada ¿por qué cortas tantas Rosas? Ella contesta
    llorosa,
Son para mi hermana Rosa. Y donde esta mi Tía Rosa?
Tu Tía Rosa es una mariposa que al cielo se me fugo.

(One early morning I was with my dear mother in the garden
While she was cutting a bouquet of roses with her scissors.
Astonished I asked her, why are you cutting so many roses?
Tearfully she answered, They are for my sister Rosa.
And where is my aunt Rosa?
Your aunt Rosa is a butterfly who got away and flew to heaven.)

At the last Nochebuena my mother and I celebrated in 2010, I recorded her reciting her poem about Rosa on my iPhone. I have it with me always as a remembrance of Mamá, her sister Rosa, and my mother.

4

My Grandfather's Picture

My grandfather
Miguel Angel
Gongora with my
cousin Alicia Elena

As usual, about a week later, I went to see how my grandmother was. I would take the same trip down Snake Hill and ring her doorbell. She would give me the usual snack, a rolled-up piece of ham and Munster cheese, and we'd sit on her sofa ready story about Cuba to be told. Then she would say, "Did I ever tell you about the time . . ."

I interrupted Mamá this time. Not ever meeting my grandfather and not knowing why Mamá and my grandfather separated, I was still curious to see what my grandfather looked like. "Do you have a picture of Abuelo Miguel Angel?"

She said, "Wait a minute." Then she went into her bedroom and came out with a small picture. She sat down and handed it to me. "This is your grandfather."

I asked, "Who's the young blond girl with him?"

"That's my granddaughter Alicia Elena, your Aunt Silvia's daughter."

"Where are they? I've never met either of them."

"Your grandfather died in Cuba a few years ago, and Alicia Elena still lives in Cuba, along with your Tía Silvia and Tío Pancho" (*tía* and *tío* mean "aunt" and "uncle" in Spanish.)

I remember my Tía Silvia and Tío Pancho. They used to come visit every winter. Tía Silvia loved the snow. She was so much fun because as soon it would snow, she would take us all sleigh-riding. I have so many great memories of my Tía Silvia and Tío Pancho's trips to New York. We went to the Bronx Zoo, the circus at Madison Square Garden, and Radio City Music Hall. I remember my brother Bobby, he was seven at the time, being a wise guy by asking my mother, "Are Tía Silvia and Tío Pancho our bodyguards? They go everywhere with us."

They all laughed

I also remember when I was five years old Tía Silvia wore a delicious perfume in her hair that smelled like some exotic tropical flower. I would sit on Tía Silvia's lap just so I could smell her hair. When I would do that, my mother and my aunt would laugh hysterically.

Tía Silvia even knew songs in English. I remember her singing, "I love coffee, I love tea. I love the boys, and the boys love me."

"How did Tía Silvia know how to speak English?" I asked.

"When she was a little girl, I sent her and your Tía Marta to a Catholic boarding school in Pennsylvania."

"My mother went to boarding school too, right?"

"Yes, I sent her because she wouldn't obey me. Did I ever tell you about the time I chased her all over the ranch?"

"No, why?"

"Because she was impossible and wouldn't listen to me. It was my fault. Your mother is the youngest of my nine children, and I spoiled her. She was so pretty and too smart for her own good."

"But why did you chase her?"

"After we moved to Santa Felicita, our cattle ranch, I started holding classes for my children and all the children in the area. My class began at 8 A.M., right after breakfast on my dining room table. This one day, all the children were sitting and waiting for me to start my class. Everyone was on time except for your mother. Your mother was seven years old at the time.

"I started calling for her, and she would yell out 'I'll be there in a little while, Mamá.' But she would never show up to class. This happened almost every day. One day, I had had enough and I went outside to try to convince her to come in. But to no avail. Every time I attempted to grab her by the hand, she ran and got away. This put me in a very difficult position. I had to do something about her education, and this is why I decided to send her to boarding school."

"My mother never told me why you sent her to boarding school, now I understand why. But why didn't my Tía Silvia, Tío Pancho and their daughter come to the United States?" I asked.

Mamá responded "The reason Silvia and Pancho didn't come to the United States is because Alicia Elena is their only daughter, who is married to Enrique, who is pro-Castro."

"You mean they're communists?"

"You might say that. I don't interfere with their political choices even if I don't agree. But what makes me sad is they are not allowed to come to the United States, not even to visit. Who knows if I'll ever see them again? My son Mario, your uncle, still lives in Cuba too, with his wife and seven children."

"Is Tío Mario a communist too?"

"Oh, no. Your Tío Mario is anti-Castro."

What a relief I felt hearing that not all my family in Cuba were communist. When I was growing up, *communist* was a very scary word for me. In school all I ever heard was that the Russians were communists and were threatening to drop a nuclear bomb on the United States. We also had practice drills to go under our desks in case of an invasion, and there were fallout-shelter signs everywhere.

Many years later, as an adult and living in Houston, Texas, I was invited to a dinner party in Kingwood, which was about an hour away. The hosts were a Cuban woman named Elena and her Texan husband, Bill. I arrived and said my hellos. Then Elena took me to the kitchen to meet her mother.

Her mother said, "I understand you're Cuban. What part of Cuba is your family from?"

"My mother is from Camagüey." Camagüey is a township in north-central Cuba.

She said, "So am I. What is your family name?" To Cubans, family names are very important.

"Peraza was my grandmother's name," I said, knowing the name was well-known.

But she said, "I don't know any Perazas."

"Actually, my mother's maiden name is Gongora."

She said, "I had a very good friend named Silvia Gongora. She was so much fun. She told jokes, pulled pranks, and she always made us laugh."

I couldn't believe my ears. "That's my aunt—Tía Silvia!"

"This is amazing," she exclaimed. "All the way from Camagüey to Kingwood, and here we are. You know your Tío Pancho worked side by side with my husband at the Royal Bank of Canada? We were all such good friends. Those were the good old days, before that monster came into power. I don't understand how anyone could stay in Cuba and support him," she said, referring to my aunt and uncle. That was the end of the conversation in Kingwood.

I never learned any details regarding my grandparents' separation. But I was still curious about my grandfather and what he was like. Since Mamá didn't volunteer any information about their separation, I didn't dare ask why they separated. I certainly wasn't going to pry about how my two aunts tarnished the family's reputation.

5

Cuban Palm Trees

Mamá's paintings of Cuba

Right across from Mamá's sofa hung two of her oil paintings, Cuban landscapes that she painted a long time ago, when she still lived on the island. I couldn›t believe that my grandmother could actually paint something so realistically. I wanted to paint like her. When Mamá realized my interest in art, she gave me my first drawing lessons. Whenever I went to visit Mamá, I would always go to her paintings and stare at them in awe, hoping that someday I would be able to paint like her. But it wasn't just the beauty of her art, it was Cuba. I would drift off to the beautiful beach with the swaying palm trees and pretend I was there. I dreamt of someday going to Cuba to see these palm trees in person.

This one afternoon, I asked, "When did you paint these paintings?"

"Did I ever tell you about that time? Well, I hope I remember," she said.

"You remember, Mamá," I said.

"Oh yes. It was in the late afternoon. I had my *pamela* on."

"What's a *pamela*?"

"It's a straw hat with a wide brim that could shade my face from the sun. I was at the back of the house, out in the field. My easel was set up, my paints mixed, and I had just made some new paintbrushes from my horse's tail."

"You made your own paintbrushes from your horse's tail? *You had your own horse?*"

"Oh yes. We all had horses. There were no cars back then, and it would take too long to get paintbrushes by mail. Anyway, the back of the house was my favorite place to paint. I painted there on most afternoons." My grandmother was born in that house on a sugar plantation in Sagua la Grande, a township west of Camagüey.

Then I asked, "Mamá? Did you love Abuelo?"

"Oh yes very much. We were both very much in love." said Mamá.

"The day I finished that painting," she continued, pointing to the one on the left, "was the day your grandfather Miguel Angel came to me and said, 'You are as beautiful as your paintings.' He was very handsome, but I was afraid to encourage him because I knew my parents would not approve of him."

"Why?" I asked.

"Because he was one of my father's workers. My parents expected me to marry a man of position, an aristocrat. That's my father in this picture," she said, obviously changing the subject and pointing to a photograph of a big man in the oval frame. "Florencio Francisco de la Caridad Peraza, your great-grandfather. He died many years ago."

"What was it like growing up on a sugar plantation?

Mamá answered. "It was wonderful. Our house was beautiful, it was like living in a small town with everyone you loved."

"Did your father have slaves?"

"Yes, but not while I was growing up. Even then, my father was very kind to his workers and paid them very fairly. Slavery is something we can never feel proud of. It all began with our ancestors, the four Peraza brothers from the Canary Islands, who came to Cuba in the 1700s to open sugar plantations. No, actually, it started before that, in the Canary Islands. The Perazas conquered the Canary Islands, and became their king and queen. Their monarchy didn't last, so they went into the sugar business."

"Our ancestors were kings and queens of the Canary Islands?"

"Yes. Someday, I'll tell you all about them."

"Wow, we come from royalty, and I have communist cousins." I kissed my grandmother goodbye, and off I went.

6

This Can't Be True

Tía Silvia and Tío Pancho with my sister Nancy in Central Park, 1953

When I got home, I told my mother, "Mamá said that our ancestors were the king and queen of the Canary Islands. Did you know that?"

My mother replied, "Yes, I heard that, but that's all I know"

"Did you also know that Tía Silvia's daughter, Alicia Elena, was married to a communist?"

My mother said, "Yes, but you must not repeat that."

I said, "Okay, but why?"

"Because the Cubans that are in the Unites States hate Castro and the communist system. It's just better if we don't talk about this."

"Mom, Tía Silvia and Tía Marta went to Catholic boarding schools like you, except their school was in Pennsylvania."

"Yes, my school was in Camagüey. Although my school was closer to home, they didn't go through what I went through. Besides, they had each other. I was alone."

"So, Mom, Mamá said you weren't such a good girl when you were little. Did you get punished, or spanked?"

"Are you kidding? I got away with murder!"

"Then how come you are so strict with us? We would never disobey you. You'd kill us."

"That's because I don't want you to go through what I went through."

"So, what happened to you?"

My mother began to explain. "Imagine having everything you ever wanted. I grew up on a cattle ranch. It was so beautiful. It was called Santa Felicita. The land went for miles and miles. I never was able to reach the end. As you entered Santa Felicita, you came down this long road that was flanked with majestic *palmas reales*—royal palm trees. The road was at least two miles long. At the end, on the left side, was our house, and just before you reached the house, on the right was our dairy barn where Mamá used to make fresh buttercream and cheese."

"How big was your house?"

"It was a huge house that had a porch that wrapped around the entire house."

"How many bedrooms were there?"

"There were six bedrooms divided by a wide corridor. Each room had windows as tall as doors that opened onto the porch. At one end of the corridor was the living room, and at the other end was the dining room, the most important room of the house. It had a long mahogany table with twenty tall, cane-backed chairs. That was where we ate every meal."

"Where were the kitchen and the bathroom?"

"There was a very big bathroom off the living room. It had pretty green tiles. The kitchen was off the dining room, in a separate building that also housed the servants."

"You had servants?"

"Oh, yes. There was a cook, someone to clean, and someone to do the laundry. There was also Lina, my nanny. I loved her so much. I still think of her to this day."

"Gosh, I think if we had just one maid, it would be great."

"We all had our own horses. I loved my Bandurita. She was a small horse. They gave her to me on my sixth birthday. I also had two beautiful white chow chows. They were like my dolls. Almost every afternoon, I would bathe them and comb their hair."

"What were their names?"

"Dickie and Rebecca. When I was seven years old, I learned how to cook *arroz con pollo* right there on a real coal stove in my own little thatched-roof house. My father was my first dinner guest."

Hearing about her life at Santa Felicita, with horses, servants, and their big house with all those rooms, I couldn't help but make the comparison and wonder why I was living with my parents along with my six brothers and sisters, squished into a two-bedroom apartment in Washington Heights. My living conditions were a stark contrast to my mother's upbringing.

My mother continued, "This was the happiest time of my life. Unfortunately, it didn't last."

Then my mother began to tell me about one of the saddest days of her life.

"I will never forget this day. I was seven years old at the time. The air was full of the most beautiful sweet smell from the rain shower that had just fallen. The sunset had every color of the rainbow. It looked like heaven on earth. Then out of the blue, as I was coming in to the house, my parents asked to speak to me, I wondered nervously what they were going to say. This was the first time they ever sat me down at the dining table to talk to me. My parents' faces had a seriousness I'd never seen before, except when they had talks with my older sisters.

"My mother began speaking. 'Irma, your father and I have decided to send you to the best Catholic boarding school in Camagüey, María Conciliadora. It's a great school. You will learn so much. I know this sounds very cruel now, but in time, you will learn to appreciate it. It's for your own good. You are such a smart little girl. It would be a crime not to give you a proper education. I know you'll miss us as we will miss you, but given that you refuse to attend my classes, you leave us no choice.'

"I couldn't believe my ears. I pleaded with them not to send me away. I cried, I begged, and I even promised to go to my mother's classes. But their decision was made. The next thing I knew, I was packing to go to boarding school."

"How long did you go there?"

"I was now fifteen years old and had been away for eight years, except for vacations. I hated it; I was so unhappy. All the nuns were Italian and mean, with a couple of exceptions. The food was horrible, and they forced me to eat that junk. I do have to admit that my parents were right. I did get a good education, and they taught me to be disciplined."

I thought to myself, *How horrible*; and said to my mother, "No, thank you! I love PS 189 and sleeping on a high-riser in the living room and having you and Pop and all my brothers and sisters right here in Washington Heights."

My mother continued, "The worst day of my life was yet to come. I was so happy and excited to finally graduate and go home to my beloved Santa Felicita, But I knew something strange was going on because your Tía Silvia and my brother-in-law Pancho were outside the principal's office. They had come to take me home. I asked them, 'Why didn't Mamá and Papá come to pick me up?'

"Silvia said, 'They stayed back to prepare your welcome-home party.'

"The sad truth was I was going home to very bad news. When I reached my house, I saw my mother on the front porch, rocking herself and crying. I asked her why she was crying. She told me that my oldest brother, Miguel Jr., had passed. He was only nineteen years old.

"I started to scream, 'What happened to my brother? How did he die? He's too young to die!'

"My mother explained, 'He was sent back from the University of Havana with tuberculosis.' In 1941, there was no cure for tuberculosis, and it was highly contagious.

"Miguel became ill through a series of events. Apparently, he was hurt quite badly by the upper classmen on the night of his initiation. It landed him in the hospital. At first, it was pleurisy, then pneumonia, which turned into tuberculosis. With no cure, the doctors recommended that he come back home to the ranch, where there was plenty of fresh air.

"'My brother is dead?' I asked. 'Why didn't anyone tell me he was sick?'

"'We didn't want to upset you at school. What good would it do? *No había remedio*.'

"Then came even more devastating news. My mother said, 'We have to sell Santa Felicita.'

"I was crying hysterically. I asked her, 'Why are you selling the ranch? What about Bandurita, my horse, and my dogs, my everything?'

"'Your father and I have decided to separate, and we are dividing our assets.'

"'But why are you and Papá separating? He loves you, and you love him. You've always looked so happy together. I will never be happy anywhere else but in Santa Felicita. This can't be true!'

"'Mamá said, 'Your father will explain it all to you when he comes home.'

"I thought, *This can't be true. Miguel is dead, and we are leaving Santa Felicita*. I ran and got Bandurita, my horse, and rode as fast and as far as I could until it got dark. My sisters Lila and Elba came and got me and took me home. They tried to comfort me, but there wasn't anything they could say that would change or relieve the pain I felt."

7

The Mistress

Santa Felicita,
my grandparents'
cattle ranch

For over forty years, my grandparents Alicia and Miguel had a storybook marriage and nine beautiful children (seven girls and two boys: Silvia, Marta, Isabel, Miguel Jr., Mario, Elba, Ana María, Lila—and my mother, Irma). Miguel Sr. became a very successful cattle rancher, and often was away doing business. There were rumors of his having a mistress. Rumors like these were common, and usually true. Most wealthy Latin businessmen had mistresses, and it was acceptable in society as long as you kept it secret from your family.

But he couldn't hide his other life any longer. The rumors were true, and far worse, he not only had a mistress, but his mistress had borne him three sons.

Upon learning this information, Mamá's life changed forever.

Mamá said to Miguel, "How could you let this happen to our family? I have been a good wife. I have given you nine children. I have supported you in every endeavor. I know I'm older and not pretty anymore, but I am the same person you married. I love you with all my heart. We have six unmarried daughters. What about their future? With no father, who is going to represent them? Nobody of any quality will want to marry them. I fought with my family to have them accept you, and now you're throwing it all away for a nobody. This is such a disgrace. I will never be able to hold up my head again. But if you insist on going to her and her sons, what choice do I have? We will separate; but no divorce, for I am a Catholic woman. God will have to take care of me."

Miguel replied, "Please forgive me. You are the most wonderful woman in the world. No one could ever compare to you. I am very ashamed of myself. I know you don't deserve this. I never expected this to happen. I always considered myself a strong man. Now I see I'm the weakest man who ever lived. I believed that because I was rich, nothing could happen to me. It's all my fault; I was away so much. I was lonely. I just thought I was satisfying my physical desires, but when she told me that I was going to be a father again, something happened to me. It was like I was young again. Before I knew it, she was pregnant with our third son. They are little boys; I need to father them."

Mamá was heartbroken and still very much in love with my grandfather, but she knew it was time to separate. So they sat down in their dining room; and in a very civil manner, they agreed to sell the ranch and split their assets.

Mamá said to Miguel, "Before you go, you must talk to our baby girl, Irma." Even though my mother was fifteen years old by then, she was still their "baby girl." My grandfather went to his humidor and got a cigar, then sat on the porch and waited for my mother to come. My mother loved her mother, but adored her father.

A servant came to my mother and said, "Your father is sitting on the porch and wants to see you."

She went and sat next to him, then asked, "Why are you and my mother separating?"

He said, "This is very hard for me to explain. But while I was away, I got very sick with my asthma, and there was a very nice woman who took care of me and nursed me back to health. We became very close, and I would visit her whenever I went to Las Tunas. We now have three sons, and I need to help her raise them so they can become good men. They need a father."

While hysterically crying, my mother said, "I'm a girl, and I need a father. I need you more than they do. Are they going to sit on your lap?"

He just put his head down, and tears rolled down his face.

My mother was the only daughter to reproach him. She never really got over it. Even as an old woman, whenever she spoke of this time, tears would roll down her face.

Divorce was not an option for Catholics back then, so my grandparents simply separated. In those days, this was a scandal. The Peraza name was tarnished, the family reputation ruined. This would make it hard to marry off her six daughters to society gentlemen. Mamá, born an aristocrat, would never again enjoy her place in society.

8

The Decision

The house in Camagüey

Mamá was now responsible for her family. With the funds from the sale of the ranch, she decided to leave the country and buy a house in the town of Camagüey. She bought a Spanish-style townhouse with a courtyard and four bedrooms to keep her family together.

My mother learned to love this house too. She would talk about the stained-glass windows, the marble columns in the living room, and the mosaic tile with a geometric design.

My mother also learned to like their new lifestyle. She and her sisters joined the tennis club. Every Saturday night, they had great dances with wonderful musicians. My mother wore a brand-new handmade dress almost every week just for these dances.

Mamá only had one son left, Mario. Mario was very handsome and a playboy, and had many girlfriends before settling down with his wife Zenaida. Mamá laughed when she told me about the time she went to Havana to see Mario at the university. When she got there, he was on the high diving board at the country club pool, ready to dive off. He did a beautiful and perfect swan dive; and when he emerged from the water, there was a beautiful girl on his shoulders.

Because of his lack of interest in school, my uncle Mario was brought back to Camagüey to help my grandmother. Unfortunately, Mario was not much help to her. Mamá tried setting up different kinds of businesses for him, but they all failed. He eventually went back to a girlfriend who lived in the country and married her, and they quickly started having one kid after another.

Mamá tried everything she could to invest her money, but nothing seemed to work. She bought rental houses, but the tenants didn't pay their rent, so she ended up selling them at a loss. She bought a grocery store, but it too failed, because it was during World War II and supplies were difficult to get. All her money was quickly disappearing, with no money coming in to support all her children.

Something had to change. That's when Mamá made her decision, and told her family that they were all moving to New York.

Most Cubans migrated to the United States post-Castro, but my family was different. They came to the United States in 1946, right after World War II. They did not leave Cuba because of political affiliations, but for other reasons.

"Mamá, it must have been difficult to leave your beloved Cuba." I said.

Her eyes suddenly glazed over, as if she were in a trance. Then she spoke thoughtfully. "I will never forget that day. It was late afternoon, during the usual mid-afternoon tropical downpour. I was in the *recibidor*, the entry parlor, rocking myself in my favorite chair and thinking, *How am I going to break this news to my family?* I gathered all my strength, walked over to my long mahogany dining room table, sat at my place at the end, and said to the maid, 'Tell my girls to come. I need to speak to them.'"

Mamá was supporting six of her daughters, along with six grandchildren and herself. Therefore, she was responsible for thirteen people. I can't imagine the weight on her shoulders.

"All at once, my girls entered and began screeching words of anticipation:

"'*Que sera?*—what's going on?'

"'Mamá, are you sick?'

"'Did someone die?'"

It all must have sounded like fire engine sirens racing to put out a fire.

Mamá continued her story. "I told them all to be quiet and to listen. Then I said, 'I made some very important decisions. Up until now, I tried not to involve you in our economic affairs, but I have no options left. We have enough money to last a year living here in Cuba, in the style to which we are accustomed.'

"They gasped as they looked at each other. Their faces froze in fear. But I continued talking. 'Given our economic situation and what has happened to our reputation . . .'

"Suddenly, Ana María blurted out, 'But why should we suffer? We did nothing wrong. Let Marta and Isabel pay! *Ellas metieron la pata*—they're the ones who disgraced us!'

"I looked at her and spoke. 'Ana María, please listen and be quiet. I have given this a lot of thought; and I think it would be best if we moved to the United States, where we could all get a fresh start. I'm sure that in time, you will all meet and marry gentlemen from fine families. Of course, in the beginning, it will be hard getting used to a new country, and leaving Cuba and everyone and everything we know. But you could even find jobs in America.' I heard Elba whisper to Ana María, 'Our situation must be really dire if Mamá is suggesting we find jobs.' Indeed, she was right.

"Up until then, the idea of them getting jobs was never even a consideration. My girls were raised as Cuban society women, and they didn't go to the university like my boys. They were groomed to marry eligible bachelors from high society. They had all been taught to play either the piano or the violin and do needlepoint. These skills weren't exactly moneymakers, and my daughters fit that traditional Cuban mold exactly. But because they were young and pretty, they probably wouldn't have trouble meeting men in America.

"But what kind of jobs could they get? That, I didn't know, and I continued, 'I know it won't be easy leaving Camagüey, our friends, our house, everything we know. It's all because of your father and that other woman . . .'"

At that moment, Mamá stopped to gather herself before she continued speaking, as if remembering what it was like to tell someone honestly what she knew to be true. "Telling the truth was very difficult, *mijo*. But I did it. I said, 'I don't see any other solution. As you know, I have tried everything to be successful with the different family businesses. I tried to make money with our rent houses and the grocery store. The truck that I purchased simply gives your brother Mario enough to support his family.'

"'I'm not going,' Irma said. 'You can all leave without me. I'll live with Silvia,'

"I told her, 'Please don't interrupt me, Irma. I will give all of you a chance to speak when I am finished talking. I plan to sell this house and everything in it. This will give us money to tide us over until we can get back on our feet. I think it is best if we go in small groups. I have thought it over very carefully. Elba, thank God you speak English. You will go first with Lila and Ana María. I wrote to my old friend Rita, who has been living in New York for the past five years, and asked her if you could stay with her while you are getting situated with jobs and a place to live.'

"'She agreed. I knew she would understand. Her plight was just as difficult as ours. Rita is such a good friend. We've known each other since we were little girls. I will forever be grateful to her.'"

Then Mamá told me, "Your mother, Irma, who was twenty at the time, defiantly said, 'No, I'm not going. I'm not leaving my dogs. I love my house, my friends, and the tennis club. No, I'm not going.' She started to cry.

"I put my arms around your mother and tried to console her. I said, 'You'll love New York. It's the best city in the world.'

"Then your aunt Elba, who was thirty years old then, said, 'This is so exciting. I'm going to meet an American and get married. I won't end up an old maid after all!'

"Your other aunts, Ana María, twenty-seven, and Lila, twenty-five, were equally happy with the prospect of meeting eligible bachelors from America. With no money and the family's tarnished reputation, their chances of marrying into Cuban society were just about gone.

"Then Marta, my second oldest, spoke up. 'What about me? I speak English perfectly. Why don't you send me first?'

"'No, you will have to go later, after we are established. And besides, I wouldn't ask Rita to take you in with your two children. It would be too much to ask, and it would be better for your sons, Norman and Roy, to come when we have our own home in New York. I suggest you shouldn't interfere. You are responsible for a lot that has gone wrong with this family.'"

Marta was absolutely gorgeous and a few years earlier had been engaged to be married to Yago, one of the most handsome young men of all of Camagüey, and the son of one of Camagüey's most prominent families. Marta and Yago made the perfect couple. Both were from well-respected wealthy families.

Unfortunately, with only three months left before the wedding, Marta had become pregnant. Upon learning this, Yago's parents had forbidden him to marry Marta. Between my grandparents' separation and Marta's mistake, this was the beginning of the demise of my family's reputation. Marta was forever labeled as spoiled merchandise. Cuban society could be really cruel, especially when a family was running out of money. And what made matters worse was that a few years later, Marta had become pregnant again, this time by her second boyfriend. As you can imagine, the disgrace was far too great to be forgiven.

Growing up, I was very close to my Tía Marta. I didn't understand why at the time, but I knew she was very sad. I spent many weekends with her, partly because I wanted to keep her company, but mostly because she was the first one in our family to have a color television. It was a treat. I watched all my favorite programs while Tía Marta worked on *The New York Times* crossword puzzle. I remember her telling me that she had become friends with Jeanette MacDonald. Tía Marta met her at the country club. I didn't know who Jeanette MacDonald was until I was much older and saw one of her films with Nelson Eddy. Tía Marta showed me a letter from her. I got the sense that she hung on to that letter as a reminder of her happy days in Cuba.

Mamá continued describing her discussion with her daughters. "I turned to Isabel and said, 'Isabel, you and your children will come later.' Isabel put her head down and didn't say a word, because she had caused another embarrassing family situation, adding to the decline of the Peraza-Gongora name."

My Tía Isabel was a second grandmother to me; she always called me her little gentleman. She was just under five feet tall, cute as a button, and missing a couple of fingers on her left hand. My mother explained that when she was eight years old, she was staying at my great-grandfather's plantation. While she was playing outside, she found a blasting cap used for explosives, which the planters employed in excavating trenches for sugarcane. It went off, and her little fingers did, too. What a pity! "Isabel had played the piano beautifully," Mamá told me.

I did not learn the details of Tía Isabel's disgrace until I was much older. Isabel had been dating one of the Bacardi men, named Gustavo. One day, she came home, hysterically crying with the news that she was pregnant. This was right after Marta's situation. To avoid any further damage to the family's reputation, her parents went and spoke to the Bacardi family. They were hopeful they could arrange a marriage and cover up this indiscretion before anyone would know. Unfortunately, Gustavo denied his involvement and refused parental responsibility. The Bacardi family apologized and said there was nothing they could do, and closed the door. The news spread like wildfire. Once again, shame and dishonor came to the Peraza-Gongora family.

But Isabel's story continued from there. She was introduced to her brother Mario's brother-in-law Antonio. Antonio was rugged and handsome, but a poor man who lived on his family's ranch. A good man, he agreed to be a father to her baby, and they married. After their wedding, Isabel moved into Antonio's bedroom in his family's house. Spoiled by all the Perazas, she never dreamed her life would turn out like this. Unsatisfied, like a spoiled little rich girl, every time she got pregnant, she would get angry with her living situation and leave her husband to go back to her parents. After each baby was born, she would forget about her previous unhappiness and return to him. And each time, with all his love, he would accept her with open arms. But after the fourth baby was born, Isabel never returned to Antonio. From then on, she cloistered herself in Mamá's home and devoted the rest of her life to her children.

Mamá continued her story. "I knew Silvia and Pancho wouldn't go to America, because Pancho was about to be promoted to President of the Royal Bank of Canada. And Mario and his wife Zenaida were about to have their fifth child, so they wouldn't leave. But *y si Dios quiere*— God willing—they would visit us often."

Mamá tried to hold back her tears and burst out crying. "I thought, 'How am I going to leave Miguel? Who will place the flowers on his grave? I'm his mother. This is my job.'" Miguel was her oldest son, who had recently died of tuberculosis.

Mamá dried her eyes with her handkerchief and regained her composure, then shrugged. "*No había remedio*—there was nothing I could do."

And with that, Mamá ended the story of her decision to move the Peraza-Gongora family to America. For the first time, it was clear to me why my family left Cuba.

9

New York–Bound

My aunt Lila

In 1946, the Peraza-Gongora exodus from Cuba got underway. Mamá began to prepare Elba, Ana María, and Lila for the journey. Each daughter was beautiful in her own way, and each had her own unique gift. Elba's attractiveness came with her charm, talent, and perseverance. Because of her strengths and because she was the oldest in the group, Mamá put her in charge. She was also the most resourceful. With any scrap of fabric, Elba could make a dress that looked like it came out of a magazine.

Ana María had a gorgeous face, but was on the chubby side. Her nickname affectionately was La Gorda, which means "the chubby one." In Cuba, nicknames were a little cruel, but they were created out of love. They wouldn't work in America today. Mamá put Ana María in charge of the money. She was trustworthy and the most frugal. She always saved her money, and hated to part with any of it.

Lila was the youngest of the three girls, and was the prettiest of all the Gongora sisters. Lila was five-foot-nine and had jet-black hair, white porcelain skin, and curves in all the right places. Her eyes were deep-set with arched eyebrows, which made her mysterious and alluring. Everyone doted on Lila and was forever telling her how beautiful she was. Lila would smile and enjoy the compliments but never really savor them. She was afraid to draw attention to herself. She didn't want to be categorized as easy because of her older sisters' ill-fated choices, but at the same time she feared putting herself in a position to be rejected. Lila knew that with her sisters' mistakes and her parents' separation, she was branded for life, without a chance to ever marry a man from a proper family.

In the Cuban society of that era, disgrace and shame were bestowed on every member of a family if anyone in the family broke the rules of the Roman Catholic Church in the case of divorce. Unlike today, all the money in the world couldn't buy you an annulment. A divorce was definitely out of the question. Divorce equaled excommunication and banishment from the Church forever, and eternal damnation to Hell. My grandparents' separation was not considered a mortal sin, but the shame was almost as bad.

Mamá and her unmarried daughters paid a severe price. From the moment of that separation, the family's position in the Church changed drastically. For generations, the Peraza-Gongora family was a benefactor, and the first pew was reserved for them and all who married a Peraza. After the family's fall from grace and lack of money, Mamá chose to wear a black mantilla covering her face, and along with all her daughters, sat in the last pew, at the back of the church. Everyone avoided bringing up the subject of my grandparents' separation. No one wanted to remind Mamá of my grandfather and what he did.

As painful and life-changing as that separation was, the most profound repercussions followed from my older aunts' indiscretions. Cuban society would never consider the younger Gongora sisters eligible to become wives for their sons. Although the family was allowed to continue its tennis club membership, it was limited for them. The club men would dance with them and sometimes might share a meal at the restaurant, but that's as far it would go. From then on, the family was ostracized and considered outsiders. They were personae non gratae. By leaving Cuba, their disgraced status would be left behind.

Before embarking on their journey, Mamá, with a very purposeful expression on her face, handed Ana María an envelope with $500. Mamá looked into her eyes and said, "Be careful, *que dios te bendiga*— God bless you. I'm not going to see you off at the train. I will see you in New York."

The rest of the family went with them to the train station to say their goodbyes. The three sisters, with their hands waving out of the train window, cried out, *"Te veo en New York*—I'll see you in New York."* My three aunts had now accepted the move to New York as their destiny.

This was the beginning of my family's exodus. Their lives as they knew it would never be the same.

Elba sat across from Lila and Ana María. They were all quiet at first during the five-hour train ride. But as the train got closer to Havana, they slowly started talking.

"I'm sad to leave Cuba, but I'm also very excited to go to New York," said Lila. "I know I'm going to meet a handsome *Americano.*"

"You'll have to learn English first so you can talk to him," said Elba.

"Finally, you're talking about men!" said Ana María.

Upon their arrival in Havana, they got into a taxi. Elba told the driver, *"El Hotel Capri, por favor."* All their reservations had been handled by Pancho, Silvia's husband.

"Let's go out dancing at Sans Souci," Lila suggested. "I heard they play wonderful rumbas and it's really elegant. All the men wear white jackets and black bow ties."

"No. We cannot spend Mamá's money on nightclubs. We have to save every peso for New York," said Ana María.

"Oh, please? Just for one night?" Elba said. "Let's go for a little while. We only have this one night here in Havana. It will cheer us up."

"Okay, but just for a little while. Our flight leaves at 9 A.M."

The three young girls danced the night away. The club was small in comparison to the Tropicana. But it was very romantic, with a wonderful band and a sleek dance floor with little round tables with lamps.

When morning came, Elba was the first one up, and shook her sisters awake: "Come on, get up! We have a flight to catch!"

They got up and got all dolled up for their first international flight on a Pan American Airways Clipper. Wearing their hats with little mesh veils and their white gloves, off they went into the wild blue yonder.

The flight took an hour and fifteen minutes. Before they knew it, they touched down in Key West, Florida. They found their way to the Greyhound bus bound for New York.

With stops along the way, they arrived in New York City three days later, wearing their best outfits and their platform shoes, and with their hair done up in pompadours. They looked like the Cuban version of The Andrews Sisters.

Rita sent two of her daughters, Chelo and María, to meet them at the bus terminal. They were ever so happy to see someone they knew from Cuba. They kissed, hugged, and cried. In their excitement, they all began to talk at the same time and laughed nonstop.

María told them, "Okay. We are going to take the subway to our house. We have to buy tokens here. They are *cinco centavos, un* 'nickel.' We will take this train, *el numero uno*, uptown. Our stop is at 181st Street."

They reached the subway and were amazed. They had been on Cuban trains, but they had never been on a subway. They got off the subway at 181st Street and headed for the escalator. They had never been on an escalator, either. There were escalators in Havana, but not in Camagüey. Camagüey was like the Texas of Cuba. Nicknamed La Tierra de los Tinajónes, or "the land of the rain jugs," it was known for lots of money, cattle ranches, and gorgeous women.

Ana María refused to get on the escalator. "*No, me muero!*—I'll die."

They all made fun of her. "You're not going to die, hillbilly!"

That didn't convince her, and she took the stairs anyway.

They arrived at Rita's apartment building tired, scared, and excited. María said, "We only have to go up to the third floor." It was a walk-up.

On the way up the stairs, Ana María said to Lila, "Do you smell what I smell?" Elba shushed Ana María.

My grandmother's childhood friend Rita greeted them warmly with hugs and kisses, and showed them this tiny room off the kitchen that had two little beds. They looked at each other and smiled, wondering how they were going to fit in this tiny room. But with gratitude, they politely said thank you and nothing more.

"One of you will have to sleep on the couch. Here, come sit down. You must be tired. Chelo made *arroz con pollo con cerveza*—chicken and rice made with beer." Chelo was Rita's oldest daughter. They all sat down and enjoyed this Cuban feast.

"*Que delicioso*. I smelled it as soon as I came into the building," said Ana María.

"So tell me, how is my dear friend, Doña Alicia? How is she holding up? It's all so sad. Never mind, I don't want to make you sad. How was your trip?" Rita asked.

"It was long, but good," Elba answered.

"My, Lila, you are so beautiful."

"Thank you, Doña Rita," answered Lila.

"We should go to bed. I'm going to find a job tomorrow," said Elba. They all laughed, as if to say, "Sure, you're getting a job on the first day." Elba continued, "The two of you can sleep in the bedroom. I'll sleep on the couch, because I have to get up early."

The next morning, Elba got up at the crack of dawn. She woke up to the smell of Cuban coffee. Chelo was cleaning the kitchen and making the coffee. Chelo had a son out of wedlock, named Luis, who lived with them also. As her penance for her indiscretion, Chelo sort of became the family maid.

"Sit down, Elba," said Chelo. "Here, have some coffee and tostadas. Here is a newspaper. They list jobs at the back. Can you read it?"

"Yes," Elba answered. After just a few minutes Elba says, "*Dios mío!*—my goodness! there is an advertisement for a seamstress. I sew very well. I'm going right now to get this job."

Elba put on her best dress, combed her hair, and off she went. "Tell my sisters I'll see them later, after I finish working." She held the ad with the address in a tight fist like it was a hundred-dollar bill. When she got to the subway, she showed the ad to the token agent and asked, "At what stop do I get off?"

The clerk answered, "28th Street. And when you get off, just walk one block south to 27th Street and look for the number 243."

"*Muchas gracias.* I mean, thank you very much."

After a half-hour on the train, she arrived at her stop. She climbed the stairs and looked around, more than a little confused. Elba wandered before she found the building in the ad, and went into the elevator.

The elevator operator asked, "What floor, ma'am?"

She showed him her ad.

"Oh, you want the seventh floor."

The elevator opened to a huge room with about fifty sewing machines zipping along. A woman came up to her and asked, "Can I help you?"

Elba said, "Yes, I'm here to work."

"I see. Can you sew?"

"Oh yes, I make doll clothes for all my nieces."

"Doll clothes? You're kidding, right?"

Elba just smiled.

"Okay, let's see what you can do. I want you to sew a seam around this fabric."

Elba sat down at the sewing machine and sewed the seam as straight as a ruler.

"Okay, come here and fill this out. The pay is two cents per piece.

Be here at 7 A.M. tomorrow. And don't be late."

Elba practically ran all the way home. She couldn't wait to give everyone the news. She knocked on the door, yelling, "I got it, I got it, I got the job!"

Lila and Ana María hugged her and cried with happiness. *"Felicidades,"* said Doña Rita. "You are quite the young lady."

Chelo and María also hugged her and said their congratulations. Chelo said, "I made a flan for dessert to celebrate. I knew you were going to get a job."

They all started asking her questions, all at the same time, getting louder and louder. Doña Rita said, "Leave the poor girl alone! Come sit next to me."

"I start tomorrow at 7 A.M. They pay two cents per piece. They call it piecework."

On her first day, Elba was at her job early and ready to work. She met a lovely lady from Nicaragua named Graciela. They became fast friends, and their friendship would last a lifetime. In no time, she became part of the team of girls. She became good friends with another girl named Edith. Edith was also thirty and single.

One day, Elba asked Edith if she knew of any other jobs for her two sisters that didn't entail sewing.

"Yes. As a matter of fact, a man from the fifth floor asked me if I wanted to work at his electrical factory, putting these little units together. He pays three cents a unit. Not bad. Do you want me to ask him?"

"That would be so nice. Thank you," Elba said.

Soon after, they all were working in the same building. Elba now had two good friends, Graciela and Edith. One day during lunch, Edith turned to Elba and said, "I bet my brother Glenn would like you."

Elba answered shyly, "Where does your brother live?"

"New Orleans. That's in Louisiana."

"How would I meet him? Isn't that very far?"

"Give me a picture of you, and I'll send it to him. You never know."

"Okay, I'll give you one tomorrow."

A week later, Elba received a letter from Glenn. He included a photo of himself. Elba liked what she saw, and the fact that he owned properties added to his attractiveness. They continued to correspond back and forth, which was the dating system of the time. A romance began through the mail.

After six months of correspondence, Glenn asked if he could come and meet her. Elba, who was the most proper of all the sisters, responded, "Yes, I would like very much to meet you, but my mother has not arrived yet. She's still in Cuba."

He wrote back, "I'm not very patient, but of course I understand. I'll do my best because I really think *usted es muy bonita*—you are very pretty."

She wrote back, "I really like when you write in Spanish. How did you learn how to do that?"

He answered, *"Yo vivi en Cuba con mi familia cuando yo era niño."* He had lived in Cuba as a child with his family! Now Elba was really excited to meet him. But she wanted to wait until her mother arrived.

Every morning, the three sisters rode together on the subway to work. On one of these mornings in the elevator at work, as Lila and Ana María were getting off at their floor, a man turned to Lila and asked her if she were a model. She politely answered, "Oh, no. I work at the electronics company on the fifth floor with my sister."

He said, "I have an idea. Why don't you stop by my company after you finish work?" Noticing that Lila looked frightened, he added, "It's all right. You can bring your sister. I'm on the tenth floor. My name is Mr. Goldsmith."

She smiled, and said in a shy voice, "Okay, thank you."

Lila and Ana María got off the elevator with a little extra bounce in their step. Ana María, excited, said to Lila, "I think he wants to make you a model."

"No, it can't be. I'm not that pretty."

"Oh, yes you are!" Ana María replied.

They couldn't wait for the workday to end so they could to go up to the tenth floor to see Mr. Goldsmith. Of course, Elba was right there with them. The doors opened to a beautiful showroom. The room was lit to perfection, with Corinthian columns flanking it, like at the Pantheon. White velvet, odd-shaped sofas were placed all around the room. A shiny wood floor with a red carpet at the center led up the stairs to the stage.

This very tall woman, looking very secretarial with a bun on her head and pointy glasses, came up to them and asked, "May I help you?"

"These are my sisters Lila and Ana María, and I'm Elba."

"Yes, but how can I help?"

Just then, Mr. Goldsmith entered and said, "They're here to see me. It's okay. Come," he gestured. "Sit down. My, you are all so pretty."

He said to Lila, "Can you come here and stand under the light and walk toward me?"

"Miss Bailey," he then said, turning to the very tall woman. "What do you think?"

"She's all right. With a little instruction, she'll be okay."

Mr. Goldsmith turned to Lila. "How would you like to be a model? I can't pay you top dollar to start, but I'm sure I can pay you more than what you're making on the fifth floor. How about it?"

Lila looked to her sisters for their approval.

Elba said to Mr. Goldsmith, "Yes, but what is the pay?"

"Seven dollars and fifty cents a week, and after six months, ten dollars a week. What do you say?"

"Ten dollars a week now, and twelve-fifty after three months," negotiated Elba.

"Okay. I can do that. She starts on Monday," he replied.

And so began a new career for Lila, and she loved modeling. She loved putting on all those fancy clothes. She would pretend she was back in Cuba when she was modeling her own clothes.

One day in the showroom, while she was coming down the stairs wearing a magnificent white beaded gown, she turned and saw a handsome man who resembled Rock Hudson sitting on one of the sofas. She couldn't help but notice him staring at her with a silly grin.

Miss Bailey came back to the dressing room and handed her a card. "Mr. Carlos Duran is one of our best suppliers. He wants to speak to you."

"To me?"

"Yes, you. Now hurry up. Don't keep him waiting."

"Okay, I'll be out in a minute."

She walked up to him and shook his hand. This six-foot-three-inch-tall and very handsome man said in Spanish, *"Usted es Cubana?*—are you Cuban?"

"Sí, y usted?—yes, and yourself?"

"I am from Ecuador. I would love to take you to dinner."

"I would have to ask my sisters."

"You can bring your sisters," he said, knowing very well they wouldn't let her go out alone to dinner with a stranger. Young Latin women never go on dates without a chaperone. In Lila's case, she'd have two chaperones: Elba and Ana María.

Lila couldn't wait to tell her sisters about the dinner invitation. In her excitement, she became too impatient to wait for the elevator, so she ran down the stairs from the tenth floor to the seventh floor to tell Elba her news. Both Lila and Elba ran down to the fifth floor to pick up Ana María and share the news. Lila could not stop talking about Mr. Duran all the way home.

Elba said, "Okay, that's enough already. Let's see what tomorrow brings."

Lila could hardly sleep in anticipation of her dinner date with the South American tycoon. He invited them to join him at the Chateau Madrid, an elegant Spanish nightclub.

They arrived at the club dressed beautifully and looking gorgeous. The maître d' escorted them to the best table right on the dance floor.

Carlos was only too happy to sit in the middle of these three Cuban beauties. Elba was on his left, Lila was on his right, and Ana María was next to her. Before they knew it, waiters came from every direction and swarmed the table.

"We'll have a bottle of your best champagne," Carlos said.

The master of ceremonies came to the center of the floor and the music stopped as he began to announce: "*Señoras y señores*, welcome to the Chateau Madrid. Tonight, we have a great show just for you. Los Chavales de España, Paco and María, the best flamenco dancers from Seville, and *el señor* Argueso and his magnificent orchestra."

The sisters, their eyes gleaming with excitement, couldn't wait to dance. At that moment, Mr. Duran turned to Lila, took her hand, and led her to the dance floor. They never sat down again. They danced every song until it was time to go. Elba and Ana María also enjoyed dancing with several different men, but no one was as handsome as Mr. Carlos Duran.

At one in the morning, they all left the nightclub arm in arm and laughing with joy. Mr. Duran hailed a cab and gave the taxi driver money.

"Make sure you get them home safe," he said.

"You betcha. Thanks, partner," said the cabbie.

But before he said goodbye, Carlos asked Lila, "Can I see you again tomorrow?"

"Of course," she said.

The sisters giggled like schoolgirls all the way home.

Thus, they began their new American lives. All three girls were settled in jobs, making enough money to be self-sustaining. And both Lila and Elba had marriage prospects, pending approvals from Mamá. That left Ana María with no prospects yet in sight. It seemed she was more concerned with bringing Mamá and the rest of the family over to the United States than finding a husband.

Shortly thereafter, Lila said to Elba and Ana María, "Don't you think it's time to bring Mamá and Irma to America?"

"Yes, it's time," said Ana María. "But where would they stay? We can't all stay with Doña Rita."

Elba chimed in, "You're right. Let me ask around the factory if anyone has any ideas."

The next day, Elba starting asking around if anyone knew about a room for rent. Her friend Graciela said, "I have an extra bedroom. They can stay with me. I'm only two blocks away from where you live now."

"Oh, thank you, Graciela. You are so wonderful. How much?"

"Don't worry," replied Graciela.

"No, we have money. We can pay."

"Okay, if you insist. Ten dollars a month."

"Oh, thank you! *Dios de bendiga—God bless you.*"

Elba couldn't wait to share the news, but she waited until they were home. "Everyone, come sit down. I have wonderful news. My friend Graciela has agreed to rent Mamá and Irma a room for ten dollars a month. She lives just two blocks away from here, she's from Nicaragua and speaks Spanish. Isn't that great?" she asked.

"*Que Bueno!*" said Doña Rita.

They all hugged and cried with happiness.

"Let's call Mamá right now," said Ana María.

10

Mamá and My Mother Arrive

The Dykman Street subway station at Nagle Avenue

Mamá arrived in New York City with my mother, Irma, one month after her daughters had left Cuba, and they traveled exactly the same way. They both moved in with Graciela, my aunt Elba's friend from the factory.

At the time, my mother, the youngest daughter, was twenty years old and very spoiled. Until now, all mother knew was her privileged life in Cuba, the splendiferous tropical island. Upon seeing New York for the first time, she turned to Mamá and said, "I can't believe how ugly and dismal New York is. I want to go back to my house, my dogs, my friends. I'm going back to Cuba. I hate it here!"

But there was no turning back. For the next few days, Graciela and Mamá took my mother everywhere and did their best to cheer her up. They took her to Radio City Music Hall, the Bronx Zoo, and Central Park. But my mother was still unhappy until she met their next-door neighbor, Gloria. She and Gloria became instant friends, and their friendship would last for the rest of their lives.

Soon after they met, my mother told Mamá and Graciela about her new friend. Graciela said, "Gloria's sister Carmen and her husband Charles lived in this apartment before me. They lived here until they divorced. Apparently, their fights were loud and ferocious."

"How horrible!" my mother said.

One day, while my mother was next door visiting Gloria, a very handsome man in an Army uniform came into the apartment. He said to Gloria's husband, Artie, "Who's that little girl?"—referring to my mother. He was thirty-three and had recently returned from the war.

"I'm no little girl. I'm a woman!" my feisty mother replied.

That was all he needed. Sparks started to fly. By the end of the evening, they were making plans to go on a date.

But there was one problem. Well, there wasn't just one problem, there were several problems. It turned out Charles was the same guy who had previously lived in the apartment next door and who constantly fought with his wife Carmen before finally getting divorced. But it was even worse: before he had married Carmen, he'd been married to Minita, with whom he had a daughter, Lillian.

Getting Mama's approval would not be easy, and my aunt Ana María would also challenge the idea, since Ana María was now supporting them, and her opinion mattered. Both Mamá and Ana María opposed any possibility of Charles dating my mother.

Graciela also opposed the idea of my mother dating Charles. But my mother was determined to date him. No advice could stop her.

My aunt Elba

With World War II over, everyone was coming home to New York and looking for apartments. It was a very hard time to find a decent affordable place to live in New York City.

As usual, my Aunt Elba worked her magic and found an apartment uptown in Inwood: a two-bedroom unit on the third floor of a walk-up, renting for $38 dollars a month plus $100 key money for the super. This is where Mamá and her daughters planted their American roots. From this apartment, the destinies of the Peraza-Gongora women were gradually revealed.

Every Sunday, Mamá's living room was filled with her old friends from Cuba and eligible bachelors. One of the regulars was a very handsome man named Desi Caballero. He was from their town in Cuba. He was not interested in being a potential suitor for any of the girls; he would have been more interested in one of my uncles. Being alone in this country, he found comfort and familial love there. Throughout my life, Desi would appear at family occasions.

Once, when I was about twenty-three years old, I ran into Desi on 18th Street and Sixth Avenue. I hadn't seen him in many years. "Are you Desi?"

"Yes, that's me. But who are you?" he asked.

"I'm Ronnie, Irma Gongora's son."

"Of course! My, how handsome you've grown up."

We became friends and eventually had a brief affair, which became my secret. I visited him at his apartment in the West Village. (This was soon after I awoke to my gay sexual identity—more about that later.)

The last time I saw Desi was in his apartment in 2007. He was now well into his eighties. He had a few of his friends over, and we were all sitting around his kitchen table when he began to brag to his friends about Mamá, my aunts, and my mother. "His grandmother came from the best family in Camagüey. She was an intellectual and a fine artist. His mother and all the Gongora sisters were all beauties." Hearing him talk about my family in such a passionate way made me feel really proud to be Mamá's grandson.

Desi and I stayed friends until he died, but our lives still intersected after that. About three years ago, through a mutual friend, I was introduced to a Cuban man, Luis Santeiro. As we got to know each other, we were amazed that we hadn't ever met before. The list of friends we had in common was staggering. The list went back to our great-grandfathers who fought in the Spanish-American War. In addition, Luis's uncle lived in the same building as Desi and was his friend. Desi's memory will always have a special place in my heart.

Life for the family continued to grow on Nagle Avenue. Mamá loved opera. Back in Cuba, she listened to her favorite singer on one of those hand-cranked phonographs with the big horn on its side. Her favorite singer was Enrico Caruso. Now, she listened to her favorite arias on her electric Victrola.

Whenever my aunts and my mother got together, politics inevitably became a passionate discussion. Opera and politics, what a combination. When it got too loud, Mamá would say, "No more politics. Turn on Caruso."

That would be the cue to turn on the Victrola and set up the bridge table for the game of canasta. My aunts, Mamá, and my mother would take their places at the table, and after a few hands of cards, it would get loud again, with one of them accusing another of throwing down the card that would give her opponent a canasta. Mamá would end the game by saying, "Let's have some coffee."

Then Ana María would pass around a platter of guava paste and cream cheese on crackers, a favorite Cuban combination. Another one of my aunts would pass demitasses or little coffee cups filled with sweet Cuban coffee. When I got a little older, they allowed me to have my own little half-filled cup. There's nothing like sweet Cuban coffee. And then my aunts and my mother would light up their Viceroys. In the fifties, it was glamorous for young women to smoke. Viceroy was the cool brand of the day. They wanted to look like the stylish American women they saw in the movies. Although the smoke filled Mamá's living room, Mamá never smoked. As the smoke rose, Mamá's plan to find eligible men for her daughters started to rise, too.

Mamá's living room turned into a conveyor belt of proposals, with bachelors asking for her daughters' hands. My aunt Elba was the first daughter to receive a proposal, when Glenn, the man with whom she was exchanging romantic letters. arrived from New Orleans. When they finally met in person, it was clear that there was chemistry behind the letters. Very soon after, Glenn asked for my aunt Elba's hand. Without hesitation, Mamá gave her permission. For the rest of that Sunday afternoon, Mamá and Glenn's mother sat on the couch, making wedding plans. Elba marrying Glenn was the beginning. He was a fine young man with money. Mamá's plans for her daughters to marry well had begun to take root.

The wedding took place on July 14, 1946, at Glenn's mother's home in Paramus, New Jersey. There was plenty of Cuban and American food, with a three-tier wedding cake and plenty of champagne. Everyone had tears of joy.

The newlyweds then left to begin their new life together in New Orleans. A few Sundays after Elba and Glenn's wedding, Mr. Carlos Duran came knocking from Ecuador. He had all the qualifications: he was handsome, well-bred, and rich. But asking Mamá for Lila's hand wouldn't be so easy because, his proposal also meant asking permission to take her back to Ecuador.

On a beautiful summer day in Central Park, sitting on a bench under a majestic oak tree, Carlos took Lila's hand. "Lila, you are the most beautiful woman in the world. I know it won't be easy for you to leave your family and go so far away. But I know I can make you happy. I can give you everything you once had. We could have as many children as you like. You can come and visit your family whenever you want."

He turned to take her hand and knelt down in front of her. *"Yo te adoro. Yo quiero ser tu esposó y tu mi esposa. Te quieres casarte con migo?"*

She pulled him to her and hugged him while tears rolled down her face. She responded, *"Si. Si. Amor. Si. Si. Amor. Si . . ."*

Carlos's hand went inside his jacket pocket, pulled out a little box, and opened it. The engagement ring had a huge diamond surrounded by emeralds. "This ring belonged to my grandmother. My mother gave it to me to give to you. It's been in my family for generations. Do you like it?"

"Do I like it? It's beautiful!"

With that, he took the ring out of the box and placed it on her finger.

"I'm so happy. I will never take it off my finger, not even to sleep."

Ecuador is far from New York, but in those days, traveling to Ecuador was like going to the moon. Lila was madly in love with Carlos, and he with her. Mamá agreed to the marriage as long as he promised to bring her daughter back to New York for visits. He readily agreed.

The next day, they all went down to City Hall to witness Lila and Carlos take their wedding vows and send them on their way.

Mamá's plan was going well. Beginning with Elba and Glenn, then Lila and Carlos, the conveyor belt of marriage proposals for her daughters was in high gear. Two daughters remained unmarried: Ana María and my future mother, Irma

Ana María had gone on a few dates, but she hadn't met anyone promising. Against Mamá's wishes, Charles became a regular visitor. Every Sunday, dressed to the nines, he would arrive with flowers for Irma and chocolates for Mamá. Slowly but surely, through his perseverance, charm, and good looks, he gained Mamá's respect. Irma was mad about him.

On the other hand, Ana María totally disapproved of Charles and made her opinion known, and would not soften. One Sunday, Charles, as usual, arrived with his arms full of goodies. But this day was different. He sat next to Mamá the whole day, and just before he was ready to leave, he turned to her and asked, "Doña Alicia, may I have permission to marry your daughter Irma?"

She answered, "Aren't you too old for my daughter?" Irma was twenty years old, and Charles was almost thirty-four.

Irma listened and interjected, "He's not too old for me. I love him, and I'm going to marry him."

Sitting right there and in front of Charles, Ana María burst out saying, "You must be crazy, *loca*! He's been divorced twice! He has a daughter. No, Irma, no!!"

Mamá raised her finger to her and said, "Shush, Ana María." She then said to Charles, "Do you promise to be good to my daughter and take good care of her?" What else could Mamá say? She knew Irma would marry Charles, with or without her permission.

"Yes, I promise," said Charles.

"Okay then. I have your word, and I will hold you to it. Bring your mother over so we can plan the wedding."

Irma and Charles embraced and thanked Mamá. But as Ana María was leaving the room, she turned to Irma and said, "I think you're crazy." Ana María left the room and didn't wait for Irma's reply.

My parents, Charles and Irma, were married on December 7, 1946, the fifth anniversary of the bombing of Pearl Harbor. For the record, they stayed married until the end of my father's life in 1992, meaning they remained married for forty-six years. Not without a few explosions along the way, mind you, but they always managed to glue their marriage back together.

As for Ana María, she would not marry for many years. She devoted most of her life to taking care of and providing for Mamá. Ana María eventually accepted Charles, but she felt he would never be good enough for Irma. Whenever I would stay with her, she would make derogatory remarks about him.

12

For Better or For Worse; Mostly Better

Christmas 1952: My parents with (left to right)
Bobby, Nancy, Charlie, and me

My mother's full name was Irma Gloria Andrea de la Caridad Peraza Gongora. When she married my father, she added Torres to the list of her names. Cubans favor having long names, and the names pay tribute to their family heritage.

My mother was immediately disappointed with married life. She actually thought life would be like what she saw in Hollywood movies: all you had to do was get married and move into a big house with a white picket fence, lawn, and servants. Remember what I said earlier: being the youngest of this huge and prestigious family, she had been spoiled. Being spoiled didn't prepare her for real life. Definitively, she put her foot down and told my father that living in a small apartment would not do. My father promised her that this was only temporary, and he worked hard to keep his promise.

Soon after they married, he got a job with Elgin in Kittanning, Pennsylvania, a suburb in Pittsburgh. The company manufactured bathroom fixtures. My parents left New York City and moved into a big house on top of a hill. My mother's American dream was no longer a dream; it was a reality, just like in Hollywood movies.

Before they reached their first anniversary, my brother Charles Jr. was born. Their family continued to grow, and a year after Charles was born, my sister Nancy was born. Life for them in Kittanning was wonderful for a while. But before long, my father became restless; and my mother, who could not yet speak English at the time, was lonely and missed her family. They discussed their options and decided to move back to New York. My father started going back and forth from Kittanning to New York, trying to land a new job. On one of his trips east, he met a woman, and they became lovers.

His affair didn't stop the Torres family from growing. Upon arriving in New York my mother discovered she was pregnant for the third time. My parents temporarily moved in with Mamá and Ana María. It wasn't long before my father started coming home late; on some nights, he didn't come home at all. It quickly became very clear to everyone that he had another woman. My mother was totally devastated. She confronted him and, as she suspected, he had a mistress. She told him to leave. With shame on his face, he reluctantly left. My father's relationship with the other woman didn't last much longer, and he came back begging for forgiveness.

"I told you he was no good." Ana María informed my mother "You can't stay here forever. I'm not going to support you and your three children, like Mamá did for Marta and Isabel."

Years later, my mother said to me, "Your father was very remorseful, and promised it would never happen again. What was I supposed to do? I had two children and one on the way, and I was still madly in love with him and I didn't want my children to grow up without a father like I did, so eventually, I gave in." They moved temporarily to Union City, New Jersey, with my father's mother, Abuela Cándida our other grandmother, and that's where my brother Bobby was born. Bobby was born eleven months after Nancy, making them "Irish twins." Shortly afterward they moved back to Washington Heights, into Artie and Gloria's old apartment 6F at 523, in the same Washington

Heights apartment where they had met. That's where I was born.

Artie and Gloria had moved to a bigger apartment on 180th Street and Broadway, about seven blocks away. My parents remained best friends with them. We saw them a lot. They were Uncle Artie and Aunt Gloria to all of us. They played a very important part in our lives as I was growing up.

Uncle Artie was very good to all of us. Many weekends throughout all our childhood summers, we'd all pile into the back of his white convertible, put our towels on the burning red-leather seats, and off we'd go to the lake or to Palisades Amusement Park. We loved it when Uncle Artie visited. He would shake the silver coins in his pocket and watch us salivate, knowing that he was going to give us a few quarters.

I loved Aunt Gloria too, but for a different reason. She was my spiritual adviser. Ever since I was a very young boy, I had a lot of inexplicable supernatural experiences, like out-of-body experiences and seeing ghosts. Afraid and hoping I wasn't crazy, I went to my mother for guidance, and she would say, "Go ask your aunt Gloria, she knows about these things." Aunt Gloria's metaphysical explanations gave me solace; they were exactly what I needed to know, and they became my spiritual foundation. Today, their daughter Norma and their granddaughter Nicole refer to us as their cousins, although we are not related by blood. We have a lot fun when people ask us how are we related. The answer always baffles everyone. "My father's second wife, Carmen, was the sister of my aunt Gloria, my mother's best friend." Good luck!

My parents made a brand-new start in apartment 6F. You could tell from the pictures that they were as happy as can be. What a great time to be born. I was their love child. There are a lot of pictures of all of us together. In all the pictures, I'm always in my father's arms. I was a happy baby. My brothers and sister were happy, too. Whenever we get together, we always talk about those great Christmases, replete with incredible toys and dolls. My sister had at least ten dolls. My brothers had boxing outfits and gloves, cowboy and Indian hats and guns. You name it, we had it. My parents were once again happy along with their four children, who were all under the age of five.

13

Nochebuena

My Mother celebrates her eightieth birthday with her seven children: (from left, back row) me, Bobby, Charlie, and (front row) Debbie, Nancy, my mother, Darlene, and Denise.

In 1955, when I was three years old, we moved from apartment 6F to apartment 2B. We had outgrown 6F. It only had one bedroom, while 2B had two bedrooms, a dinette, and a balcony. But it didn't take long before we outgrew 2B as well.

It was September 28th, 1958, when on my sixth birthday, my mother was missing. She was in the hospital, having my sister Debbie. Debbie was born on my birthday exactly six years and eight minutes after me, both of us on a Sunday. I'll never forget that birthday. My mother had planned my birthday party and invited my little friends. One by one my friends rang our doorbell expecting a birthday party. My father, unprepared for a party, took my friends and me around the corner to the candy store. He sat us at the counter and ordered each of us an ice cream sundae. We felt like big-shots. That was my favorite birthday party. Thirteen months later, on November 4th, 1959, my little sister Denise was born; and seventeen years later, on July 24th, 1969, my baby sister Darlene was born. Somehow, apartment 2B, as tight as it was, seemed to work out.

Although my mother had a privileged childhood and was definitely spoiled, she did not spoil any of us, with the exception of our baby sister, Darlene. My mother was strict, intelligent, and loving, especially when it came to understanding her children. She was our mother and confidant. We all told her everything, even our most personal secrets. My mother's advice was always on the mark; she knew exactly how to make us feel better. I was always very close to my mother. My siblings always would say to my mother, "Ronnie is your favorite."

She would answer "No, Ronnie is not my favorite—he favors me. I love all my children like my fingers; they are all a little different, but I need and love them all the same."

She also taught us how to respect and love each other. All seven of us have different and unique personalities, yet get along like best friends. Still today, not a day goes by without communication between two or more of us. My mother always said to all of us, "I can't give you all the riches I had growing up, but I can teach you morals and manners, which are worth more."

My mother was also very resourceful. We always had plenty of food, new clothes for the start of the school year, new suits and dresses for Easter, and lots of toys at Christmas. I loved Christmas, especially Christmas Eve—Nochebuena—our biggest holiday. Mamá and my aunt Ana María would come to our house for dinner. It was so much fun getting ready for these dinners. I would help my mother set up everything. It was like a magic show. We would take out the aluminum folding table from behind the sofa and set it up right in the middle of the living room. Then we would surround the table with the folding chairs that came out from behind the drapes. The lace tablecloth and napkins were handmade by Mamá back in Cuba. We would smooth out the tablecloth on the table, making sure there were no bumps or wrinkles. My mother had a very special way of folding the napkins. She would fold them into triangles and put them on top of the plates like little pyramids. Very carefully, we would take the crystal glasses out of the china closet and hand-wash all of them until they sparkled. We only used these glasses on very important occasions.

My mother sat Mamá, as matriarch of the family, at the head of the table. My mother kept a special fork that only came out when Mamá was having dinner with us. The heavy silver fork was always set at Mamá's place. The fork was the only remaining piece from their silverware in Cuba. It served as a reminder of the life once lived. We always had the traditional Cuban Christmas menu: roast pork (*pernil*), black beans and white rice cooked together (*congrí*), and cassava (*yuca*). For dessert we had nougat (*turrones*) from Spain, and guava with white cheese.

After dinner, Mamá would sing songs, sketch amazing drawings for us, and look at our notebooks. If anyone of us had a good grade, she would reward us with a quarter; and when we got promoted, she gave us a dollar. We never missed showing her our report cards.

I remember my seventh Christmas. I really wanted this particular toy. It was a ferry boat with cars on it, like the Staten Island Ferry used to have. I saw it in the window of Simon's, our neighborhood toy store. Every time I passed by, I would stare at the window and just dream of having that ferry boat. I really wanted the boat more than anything. But I also knew it was expensive and my mother probably couldn't afford it.

When Christmas came, there was a box under the tree with special gold wrapping paper. There was no tag on it, so I asked my mother who this box was for. Is it for me? She said, "No, it's for your cousin Pepito." I never gave that box another thought.

On Christmas morning, my mother started handing out the gifts. She had a knack for gift-giving; everyone always got exactly what they wished for. My mother handed me the box in the gold wrapping paper. I said no; that's Pepito's gift. She said it was for me. I opened the gift, wondering what could it be. It was the ferry with the little cars.

I couldn't believe it. "The ferry is mine . . . I'm so happy. Thank you, Mommy. You're the best mother in the whole wide world!" She said, "You're welcome. You deserve it. You're such a good boy."

That was my best Christmas ever!

14

Abuela Cándida

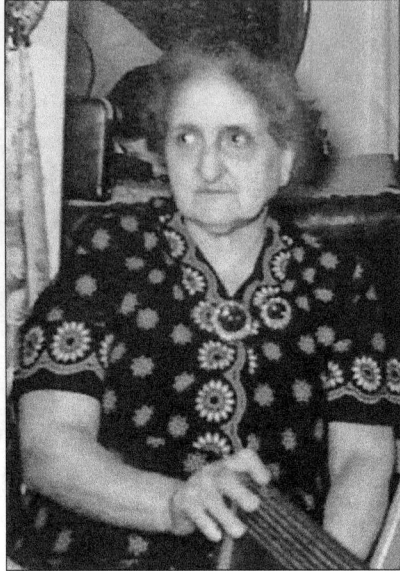

Abuela Candida,
my father's
mother

Washington Heights was very different in the 1950s. The neighborhood was predominantly Jewish and Irish, with a sprinkling of everything else. Our building, 523, was the true melting pot. We had almost every nationality you can think of, people from all over the world: Germany, Ireland, Italy, Turkey, Greece, Poland, Nicaragua, Armenia, Hungary, and of course, Cuba and Puerto Rico. But our building was mostly Jewish. Some were Holocaust survivors, with their numbers tattooed on their arms. Yeshiva University and a temple were right across the street from our building, making it easy for Rabbi Lessen from apartment 3B to go back and forth.

When I was about ten years old, I became a Shabas Goy, a non-Jewish boy who does little jobs on Saturday (the Jewish Sabbath, or Shabas) that Jews are forbidden to do because of their religion. The jobs included adjusting the air conditioner, fans, or lights. Because they weren't allowed to touch money on the Sabbath either, they would point at the table. I would lift the tablecloth, and underneath would be a quarter for me. Sometimes, Mrs. Walkenfelt, a Holocaust survivor who lived in apartment 6C, would give me chocolate too.

My family was part of the sprinkling. In those days, Puerto Ricans had a bad reputation in New York, and were the low man on the totem pole. Although my mother loved my father, his mother, and her best friend Gloria, all of whom were Puerto Rican, my mother made it clear to all of us that we were not to marry a Puerto Rican.

I would say to her, "You married a Puerto Rican, and that makes me half Puerto Rican. What's wrong with that?"

She would say, "That's different. Your father's family originally came from the north of Spain, and he's blond."

That was very confusing to me. I had black hair and an olive complexion. It made me feel ashamed of my Puerto Rican heritage. Whenever someone asked me what my nationality was, to soften the blow, I always said Cuban first, then Puerto Rican. I now feel proud to be everything I am: Puerto Rican, Cuban, Catholic, and gay.

The Peraza family contrasts sharply with my father's family. My father came from a poor family in Puerto Rico. 1928, at the age of sixteen, he arrived in the United States through Ellis Island with his mother, Cándida. In addition, his nephew Alberto and niece Judi also came, because they had just lost their mother to tuberculosis.

I was lucky to have two loving grandmothers. Mamá and my father's mother, Abuela Cándida. Because Abuela Cándida lived in my building, I got to see her every day. Abuela made the best breakfasts every Saturday morning just for my father and me, which included homemade pancakes and sausages. I remember this one time, she put butter on my pancakes and the butter melted. I wanted to see the butter on my pancakes, so I kept asking for more butter. While laughing, she kept putting more butter on the pancakes until the pancakes cooled and the butter stopped melting.

I remember asking Abuela,

"Did you put butter on the pancake? Where is it? I don't see it."

"*Si, mijo.*" as the butter melted.

"I still don't see it."

"*Si, mijo.*" She added more butter. It melted too. "I still don't see it. Where did it go?"

"*Si, mijo.*" Finally the pancakes cooled and stopped the butter from melting.

"Okay. Now I see it. Thank you."

I would also make other requests. "Abuela, please sing *Jingle Bells.*" She would start with "*Cinco peos, cinco peos,*" which means "five farts, five farts," to the *Jingle Bells* melody. Every time she did it, I would laugh hysterically. I sometimes brought my little friends to see her, just so she'd sing her version of *Jingle Bells*. Abuela made us all laugh.

Abuela was unique. She smoked cigars, and would take the cigar band that was wrapped around the cigar and put it on my finger like a ring. She sometimes babysat us when my parents went out. She was the best! We'd turn off all the lights and play blind man's bluff. She would sit there in the dark and let us wreck the apartment, and put everything back together before my parents came home. My parents never had a clue.

My mother and Abuela were best friends. They spent their days together cooking and their nights playing cards, waiting for my father to come home. One day, out of the blue, my mother told me that Abuela was sick and going to Florida. My older sister Nancy and I ran up the stairs to see her.

When we arrived, our older cousin Judi told us we could not enter Abuela's room. Nancy defiantly said, "No! We are going in to see our grandmother, and you can't stop us."

Reluctantly, Judi opened Abuela's door and showed us in. I remember feeling really scared as I walked into the room. Abuela motioned to us to come to her. She was lying there, very still and without any color on her face. She kissed us both and said to me, "Be a good boy." My cousin Judi took her to Florida the next day, that was the last time I ever saw her. A few months later, my mother told me that Abuela went to Heaven. Before she left for Florida, she told my mother, "After I'm gone, talk about me. I don't want to be forgotten." Although I was just five years old when she died, I remember her as if it were yesterday. I have kept her memory alive. I talk to my siblings about her often. My three younger sisters never met her. They were born after she passed. But through me, they have gotten to know her. I missed her terribly. I still miss her.

15

Poppy

My father's Army
picture from
World War II, 1945

M y mother insisted that we identify with our Cuban heritage. My father, Poppy, was the opposite. He identified as American, therefore he never passed on to us a strong sense about being Puerto Rican, except for Puerto Rican food and the Pittsburgh Pirates. The Pirates were his favorite team, with several Puerto Rican players, including his idol Roberto Clemente. My father, a die-hard Pirates fan, took my older brothers to a Pirates game in Philadelphia, where they met Roberto Clemente in person. My brothers never forgot how genuine and friendly Clemente was. They still talk about that today.

Back to Poppy's American roots. He came to the United States when he was just a boy of sixteen. He assimilated very quickly to New York, and within three years he graduated from Haaren High School in Manhattan, with a commercial diploma. In those days, it was a big deal for an immigrant to finish high school. Haaren High School is now one of the John Jay College buildings, which is just a few blocks from where I currently live. Today, when I pass by that building, I imagine my father as a young man, going in and out.

Poppy became a crackerjack typist and stenographer. He could type eighty-five words a minute. In 1938, both skills were very valuable. When World War II broke out, my father joined the Army. Because of his skills, and because he was bilingual, he was chosen to be one of General Eisenhower's personal secretaries, a fact I didn't learn until a year before he died.

Throughout the years my father did talk about all the different countries he visited, including England, Luxembourg, and France. Luxembourg was his favorite country, but Paris changed his life. He spoke of his nights at the Moulin Rouge. He met many beautiful French women there, with whom he traded silk stockings for cigarettes.

But there was one woman who was special to him. He continued to correspond with her throughout his time in the service. They wrote a lot to each other every day. It was a deep love affair. He saved all her letters; and before he came home, he mailed all of her letters home to his mother for her to save.

His divorce from his second wife, Carmen, was a result of those letters. Abuela's name was Cándida Torres, and Carmen was also a Torres. They both lived at 523 West 187th Street, with Abuela in apartment 6D and Poppy's wife, Carmen, in apartment 6G. He made a very careless mistake: he addressed the package with the love letters to "C. Torres." The package landed in Carmen's hands.

I got to know Carmen very well. She lived right next door to Uncle Artie and her sister Aunt Gloria. Sometimes, when I visited Uncle Artie and Aunt Gloria, I would knock on Carmen's door. I loved her apartment. She was very artsy. Her apartment was decorated beautifully. My mother never opposed my friendship with Carmen.

One time, Carmen said to me, "Imagine, you could have been my son."

I thought to myself, *No way! I'm my mother's son.*

Obviously, my father was not a great husband. But he was a proud American, and he was so American that at the beginning of every baseball game, he would make all of us kids stand at attention with our right hands crossed over our hearts and sing our national anthem. I would often see tears of pride roll down his face. He would say, "This is the best country in the world."

My father was always good to me. One of my fondest memories was when I was about five years old. On some Saturdays, I would go with him to his office on Wall Street. I would sit at an empty desk with scrap paper and bang on a typewriter until I got tired.

He was a very complicated man, and I wasn't always proud of him. In fact, in my teenage years, I loved and hated him at the same time. I sometimes thought it would be better if he didn't come home and just left us alone, not because of the way he treated me, but because of the way he treated my mother. My father always had a good job, but he also had a social life apart from us, so most of the money he made never made it home. He spent his money gambling, boozing, and on other women. He often came home really late, drunk and angry.

It was horrible living under that kind of stress, and with the anxiety of what was going to happen. He was a Dr. Jekyll and Mr. Hyde. Sometimes, he came home with flowers and perfume and apologies for my mother, and all would be wonderful. On other nights, there would be a fight. We would all try to stop him from hitting my mother. My little sisters would cry and beg him to stop. My older brothers and I would get in the middle, but nothing could stop his rage.

When I was seventeen years old, on one of those nights, my parents started to get into it. At that moment I pushed my drunk father down into a chair and held him there. The pain I was feeling for my mother led me to simply ask him, "Did you love your mother?"

Knowing very well that he adored her, he was totally dumbfounded by my question. He replied, "Why are you asking me such a question?"

"Because I love my mother. How would you feel if someone came home and started hitting your mother? What would you do?"

He looked at me and was silent. Then he put his head down, and tears rolled down his face. He never laid a hand on my mother again. I have always felt that God gave me the right words at the right time.

When I was much older, I found out much more about my father. One day, my mother decided to tell me a family secret. "I'm going to tell you something about your father so you will understand him better. Your father's real last name is Serrano, not Torres."

"What do you mean?"

"I adored your grandmother, and I would never say anything to dishonor her. She was married to a man named Torres, and they had several children together. But Torres became a very sick man and was bedridden for many years. While he was ill, your grandmother, Cándida, met Maríano Serrano, the son of a Spaniard and the richest man in their town, Adjuntas. Like your father, he was very handsome, with blond hair.

"Cándida and Maríano fell in love and had an affair. She became pregnant; in that small town in the mountains of Puerto Rico, this became a huge scandal because it was obvious that Torres couldn't possibly be the father. She was disowned and shunned by her whole family. Without any means to feed and care for your father, she was left with no choice but to put him in an orphanage. Your abuela visited him every day and brought him what she could."

That explained a lot to me. I felt sorry for him; it's so hard to imagine my father in an orphanage without his mother or family or anyone else surrounding him. My father never brought up the subject because it was most likely too painful for him to discuss. To make matters worse, his father never recognized him as his son, nor gave him his name.

Now I understood why my father had this internal pain that sometimes manifested into rage. He was a man who grew up with shame and without a father. My resentment of his unacceptable behavior gradually evaporated, along with all the bad memories. Today what stands out in my mind is his generous and loving side. It was only after I learned these facts that I forgave my father and our relationship flourished.

16

The Love of My Life

Osvaldo (right) and me having fun in Key West

In 1974, my parents moved to Florida. My father finally built the house my mother always wanted. The house had four bedrooms and two bathrooms, and was very close to my mother's family.

When they were planning the move, they assumed that I would move with them. I was planning on moving with them up until two weeks before. I suddenly realized that it was time to break away from my family. I knew it was time to let my parents figure out their life together without me. Until then, because of my father's lack of participation in our family, I assumed the role of the man of the house. I took on the responsibility of taking care of my mother and my younger sisters. I was twenty-two years old; it was time to leave the nest and start living my life. What I didn't know at the time was how much my life would change. When I told my parents I wasn't going with them, they both said, "If we had known you weren't coming, we wouldn't be moving either." When I heard this, I knew for sure that I was making the right decision.

In 1975, shortly after my parents moved to Florida, I rented my first apartment, at 485 West 187th Street, exactly one block away from 523 where we used to live. It was a magnificent studio on the top floor with an incredible view overlooking the Harlem river. The studio had a huge foyer, living room, dining room, sleeping alcove, walk-in closets, and a dressing room. The sunrises from the alcove were unforgettable. All of this for a hundred dollars a month.

I quickly made lots of friends in my new building. One warm, sunny afternoon, while I was walking my dog Cleo, I met a very tall, handsome blond Cuban man named Osvaldo, who was also walking his dog. We exchanged some small talk about Cuba, and went on our way. Somehow, I never forgot about meeting him. Every once in a while, I would wonder what happened to him.

About a year later, on a really cold night, after finishing painting my apartment, I was walking Cleo when I saw a cab pull up in front of the building across the street. Osvaldo got out of the cab and started walking toward me. My heart began to beat really fast. We talked for a little while. Excited about my newly painted apartment, I asked him if he wanted to come up and see my place. He agreed.

We sat on my new white sofa, and while we were talking, he gently put his hand on mine. I felt like I was getting electrified by his touch. He then leaned over and kissed me. I had kissed plenty of girls, but never a man.

At that moment, my life changed forever. Up until then, I had considered myself straight, and thought that I would marry a nice girl and have a bunch of kids. But there was no turning back now. I fell madly in love with Osvaldo. Although this realization was hard for me to accept at first, before I knew it, Osvaldo moved in with me.

Unfortunately, our affair didn't quite last a year. We had a silly argument, and he left. I never dreamt that insignificant spat would end our relationship, but it did. Heartbroken, I slowly moved on with my life as a gay man and started dating other people, including Mamá's old friend, Desi Caballero. But Osvaldo never left my mind.

In 1986, ten years later, I heard that Osvaldo was living in Miami. Ironically, he was living ten minutes away from my parents. On one of my trips to Florida, a mutual friend arranged for us to get together. When we met, it was like no time had passed. We spent a romantic weekend together, and it was wonderful. But at the end of the weekend, as much as we enjoyed each other, we both knew we couldn't turn back the hands of time. We both had grown in different directions and decided it was best to remain simply as friends. From then on, every time I went to Florida, we would get together.

In 1989, I called Osvaldo to meet up, but he said he wasn't feeling well. When I got off the phone, I had a sinking feeling in my stomach. I thought, I hope he doesn't have AIDS. I called a mutual friend, Pepe. My worst fear was confirmed. Osvaldo had AIDS. I told Pepe that Osvaldo had been avoiding me, but that I would really like to see him somehow. Pepe lived in the same complex as Osvaldo, and planned a dinner so I could see him. I was dreading the idea of seeing Osvaldo sick. I had seen too many of my friends suffer through AIDS and die a horrible death. I lost over forty friends to that horrific disease.

Osvaldo came through the door looking as handsome as always, wearing a pink shirt and a tan. He looked the same with the exception of being a slightly thinner. We all enjoyed the dinner, just like old times. A couple of months later, on December 16th, his birthday, I visited Osvaldo. We sat in his living room and started to talk. Osvaldo advised me to be really careful about protecting myself against the AIDS virus. I reassured him that I was negative, and planned to stay that way. I asked him, "did you love me as much as I loved you?" He said, "Yes, you were the only one I ever brought home to meet my family."

Osvaldo, the love of my life, died in 1990 on Valentine's Day.

17

Lillian

My sister Lillian

I went to Florida to visit my family as often as I could. I never missed a Christmas. My father would make a big deal about me coming and would count down the days till my arrival. He would say to my mother and my sisters, "In six days, Ronnie will be here." The next day, "In five days, Ronnie will be here." When the day would finally come, my parents and my sisters would pick me up at the airport, and we would drive directly to the Christmas tree tent so I could pick out our tree. I'd always pick the fullest and tallest tree our living room could hold. When we got home, my father would pour himself a drink and sit in his favorite chair, and watch me decorate the tree.

When I was done, he would say, "Okay, Ronnie, now I want my song!" I would start singing *My Way*, then *O Holy Night*, and other carols. For my finale, he would want me to sing *My Way* again.

My father was my biggest fan. He would say, "I don't understand why you're not famous; you're better than all those famous guys."

Every Christmas, my father would say, "I'm so happy to have all my kids together. But I wish Lillian were here." (Lillian was my sister from my father's first marriage.) When he said this, I would feel sad, and also wished Lillian could be there with all of us to enjoy Christmas. I had always thought of Lillian as my sibling, even though I had never met her. But that would soon change.

One night the following year I went back to my old building at 523, to visit my friends. As I was walking through the lobby, I noticed a letter on the floor. Since I knew everyone in the building, I thought to myself, I'll pick it up and bring it to the recipient. I suddenly noticed that the envelope was addressed to my father and the return address was from Puerto Rico. Coincidentally, it was from my half sister, Lillian. I couldn't believe my eyes. I immediately called my father with the news, and he told me to open the letter and read it to him. In the letter Lillian said that her mother had told her, when she was a little girl, that he had died in the war. Lillian included her phone number in the letter, and my father called her that very night. They were on the phone for hours. In this phone conversation Lillian explained how she got his address.

Lillian met Olga, an old friend of my father's, at a party. As they began talking, Lillian learned that my father wasn't dead, and was instead married with a bunch of kids living in Manhattan. That is how Lillian got my father's address. Shortly after the phone call, Lillian, at the age of thirty-seven, was finally going to meet her father. She and her family flew in from Puerto Rico to Florida. Lillian was married to an engineer and had a son and a daughter. At the airport, when we met Lillian, we all commented how much she resembled Abuela Cándida and my sister Debbie. Lillian's daughter, Lillybell, looked a lot like my sister Denise, and both of Lillian's kids were blond like my father. Although Lillian grew up without her father, I was happy to hear that she had three uncles who didn't have children of their own and gave her everything—including clothes from Saks Fifth Avenue, piano lessons, and a college education. Lillian played the piano beautifully and was fluent in three languages: Spanish, German, and English. Lillian and my mother became instant friends. Lillian called my mother Mima, a term of endearment for "mother." From then on, she and her family spent every Christmas with us. Lillian and I became very close, as if we had actually grown up together.

18

Eight Apartments on Nagle Avenue

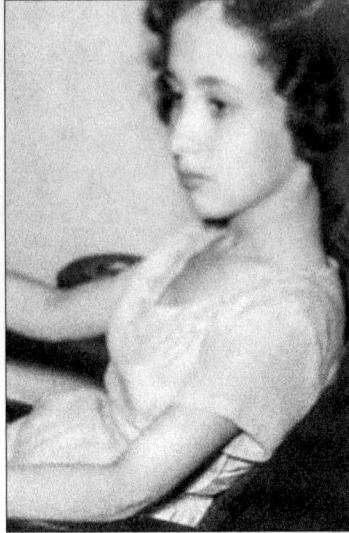

My cousin Alba

By the early 1950s, most of Mamá's family had left Cuba, and was living in New York (on Nagle Avenue) in eight different apartments, except for my aunt Isabel, who lived around the corner. Tía Isabel kept her little apartment impeccable. Her son, Armando, lived with her until he married Pucha, a nice and full-figured Puerto Rican woman. My cousins Armando and Roy were my father's drinking pals. They spent many nights at our house until the wee hours, until Roy met his wife Rosa, who was also Puerto Rican. Of course, Roy and Rosa got an apartment right on Nagle Avenue.

Tía Isabel had two other daughters besides Magaly: Gisela and Alba. Gisela lived on the ground floor with her Ecuadorian husband, Ignacio. Although I loved her very much, she was not my favorite. Alba was everyone's favorite. She was kind and sweet, like an angel.

I remember in 1962 when I was about ten years old, my mother took me and my sisters to visit Alba at her apartment on Nagle Avenue.

While there, Alba gave me three dollars—one for me, and one for each for my little sisters, Debbie and Denise. I went to the corner candy store with the three dollars. In the store window I saw these cool sunglasses. I went in and asked, "How much are the sunglasses?"

"Three dollars," replied the man.

I said, "I'll take them." Off I went looking cool with my new sunglasses.

When I got back to Alba's house, she and my mother were sitting and talking. My mother noticed my sunglasses and asked, "Where is your sisters' money?"

Caught and totally ashamed that I had spent my dollar and my two sister's dollars, I started to cry. My little cousins who were there, couldn't understand why I was crying.

Alba, recognizing my embarrassment, explained to her kids that I was a good boy who felt bad for what I did. She hugged me and gave each of my two sisters another dollar. Alba made me feel forgiven.

In the summer of 1963, when I was eleven years old, I went away to St. Vincent de Paul summer camp in Rockland County, New York, as I did every summer. This summer was different. My cousin Alba was very sick with cancer. I was very worried and scared to leave. I was afraid she might die. While I was away, I wrote home every day, but no one ever wrote back, which made me worry even more. After being away for two weeks my mother greeted me at the bus stop. Very worried an anticipating bad news about Alba, the first question out my mouth was, "How is Alba?"

My mother began to cry and told me, "Alba is in heaven." We both hugged and cried.

This was the first death I had experienced. I couldn't understand how someone so good could die so young. She was only twenty-six years old. I remember spending sleepless nights wondering if any of her habits caused her this illness. I couldn't come up with anything. Alba lived a very healthy life devoted to her children and husband. She never smoked or drank. Nonetheless, cancer got the best of her.

19

House Party

My aunt Ana
María (Tiana)

In 1964, I turned twelve years old. Almost every Saturday night my parents threw these impromptu house parties at our apartment. The guests included neighbors and relatives. My aunt Ana María—whom we called Tiana, short for Tía Ana—was a regular. I couldn't help but notice how gorgeous she had become. No longer chubby, my aunt was now a cross between Sophia Loren and Suzanne Pleshette. She wore the latest fashions, her hair in a beehive, and her makeup was always perfect. Although she had blossomed, she was still unable to find a husband.

Everyone assumed Tiana would remain an old maid, but that all finally changed the night my father invited one of his cronies from Wall Street, Juan Enrique Acevedo.

Besides Tiana, some of our neighbors from our building would also come over. Our neighbor from apartment 2E, Betty Thomashkin was always the first to arrive. She spoke perfect Spanish because her first husband was Cuban, and she had spent a lot of time in Cuba. We never knew what happened to husband number two, Thomashkin. The only thing we knew about him was that he was Russian. Betty's apartment, which was right down the hall, was always elegantly decorated. I learned a lot about decorating from her.

Kay Ratkowski, a widow from Pittsburgh, lived in apartment 1A. She was always flirting with all the men, and loved to laugh and say, "H-o-n-e-s-t-l-y, dear God in heaven."

My best friend Ray Griffiss lived in apartment 5B with his parents. His mother Bessie was an annoying busybody and sourpuss. She never bothered to knock; she would just barge right into our kitchen and lift the lid to see what my mother was cooking.

My father would say to her, "Bessie, what are you doing?"

She would answer, "Nothing, I just wanted to see what Irma was cooking."

He would tell her, "I don't like that. Don't be so nosy."

That didn't stop her. She would wave her hand down and say, "Oh, Charlie."

My father was annoyed by Bessie being a busybody, but that didn't prevent him from inviting her and her husband to our parties.

Also at the party were the McCormacks from 6B, along with their daughter Ana and granddaughter Sheila. They lived on the sixth floor, right down the hall from where my parents met. They had "adopted" my mother right after she arrived from Cuba; she became another daughter to them. I considered them my Irish grandparents. I called them Mamá and Papá. Every St. Patrick's Day, my sister Denise and I called each other to remember our Irish grandparents. The parties always began with my father serving special drinks for the ladies, such as "pink poodles"; and my mother would serve special Cuban party appetizers, including *pastica* on white bread (cut diagonally with the crusts cut off) and ham croquettes.

At these parties my parents danced to Perez Prado's cha-chas and Benny Goodman's swing music, and slow danced to Perry Como. My father and mother would rumba all over the living room floor as if they were at the Copacabana. The non-Latin women would try to drag their husbands up to rumba, to no avail.

Eventually, my father would dance the rumba with all the ladies. He was a great host. My father also loved to sing (he really couldn't, but he was still able to put over a song). His favorite song to sing was *Too Young*, by Nat King Cole; he would get very sentimental, with tears in his eyes, while he sang it to my mother. On the other hand, my mother had a beautiful voice but she was very shy. With a lot of coaxing from my father, she would eventually sing her favorite Spanish song, *Júrame*, and then in English she would sing *You'll Never know*.

It didn't end there. My father also thought he was a comedian. He would tell the same jokes every time. After a while, even before he started a joke, everyone would start laughing because they knew what was coming. Then it would turn into Ted Mack's *Amateur Hour*, presenting the von Trapp kids. That was us. We had to sing or dance or do something. My father would become the emcee, and he loved hearing us kids perform. He would often invite his office friends to these parties as well.

On this particular Saturday night, he invited Juan Enrique. He was a tall, well-dressed Puerto Rican man with an Errol Flynn mustache. I got very excited when he asked Tiana to dance. They danced every dance for the rest of the night. Throughout the evening, Juan Enrique sat right next to Tiana. They seemed to get lost in their conversation as if no one else was in the room. I could feel the buzz. Love was in the air. I had always felt sorry for Tiana because she didn't have a husband or kids, but things were now looking up. For the next several Saturdays, Tiana and Juan Enrique were regulars at our parties. Finally, he asked her to marry him; and she said yes.

The whole family was ecstatic to see Tiana finally happily married. After they got married, my new uncle moved into Tiana's apartment. Actually, it was Mamá's apartment. Mamá was happy to see her only remaining single daughter married at last, but she didn't like the idea of sharing her home, especially with a son-in-law she hardly knew. But what could she do? Mamá was old and dependent on Tiana. So, after the wedding, Juan Enrique moved in.

20

Caroga Lake

Caroga Lake, 1965: (from left, back row) my mother, me, Tiana,
and (front row) my little sisters Debbie and Denise

Tiana and my new uncle Juan's marriage was moving along smoothly. They looked so happy. In their first summer together, they planned a vacation. They rented a cabin on Caroga Lake in upstate New York, and invited Mamá, my mother, my little sisters—Debbie and Denise— and me to go along. My father couldn't go. He had to work, and my older sister and brothers thought it would be boring. They thought they were too old to go. I, on the other hand, was thrilled to get out of the city. I couldn't wait to go, but unfortunately, we weren't scheduled to go for another two weeks.

Finally, the day came. It was a really hot day in August, and I couldn't wait for them to pick us up. I waited impatiently in front of our apartment building, looking at every car that went by until Tiana's black Dodge Dart arrived. At last they were here. We all got in the car. Mamá and my mother and sisters all sat in the back. I sat in the front seat, between my aunt and my uncle.

My uncle sat behind the wheel. He had just gotten his driver's license, and even though my aunt drove to work every day, she was petrified to drive. They were both horrible drivers. The directions were written out, I was the navigator, and off we went.

We started up the New York State Thruway. The road was hot, and I was sticking to the red-leather seat. The only air came from the rolled-down windows. Finally, we stopped at the rest stop and got some cold drinks and lunch. We got off at Exit 27 and continued on small roads that passed through Gloversville and Johnstown to get to Caroga Lake.

After many forks in the road, we went through the last one. We bore left at the Acme Market, just as the directions said, and finally arrived at the hunting cabin.

The hunting cabin was old and rustic. There were all kinds of instructions on how to get the electricity and water going. It took my aunt and uncle hours to get it to work. All I wanted to do was swim in the lake. Finally, they got everything to work, and we all walked down the wooded trail to the lake. I was the first one to dive into the lake. The water was perfect. We stayed at the lake for hours. When the sun began to set, we headed back up the trail.

We swam in the lake every day. My mom, who was a great cook, made all the meals, and I helped with the dishes.

One evening after dinner, when we were all sitting on the front porch, Mamá said to my mother, "It's time for you to hear how my mother died." My mother had never wanted to hear how her grandmother died because it would make her cry. But my Mamá was now eighty years old, and wanted to make sure my mother heard the story directly from her. I sat there listening with great anticipation.

My grandmother's voice began to quiver as she told us the story. "I loved my mother so much, and I still miss her to this day."

"Her name was Cerila, right?" I interjected.

My mother turned to me. "That's right. How did you know that?"

"Mamá told me. She's in the picture on the wall in Mamá's hall. And her husband was named Florencio."

My mother said, "Soon, you'll know more about our family than me." The only thing we knew about Cerila was that she had died very young.

My mother asked Mamá, "What was your mother like?"

Mamá continued, "She was very loving and affectionate, but always very proper. She wanted to make sure that I would marry well. She secured meetings with all the right possible suitors. Every Sunday after church, she would invite these young men to our house for coffee and pastries. They would bring me flowers and recite poems. Some would even serenade me with Spanish guitars. But somehow, none of these eligible young men from proper families ever caught my attention. Whenever I thought of love, I thought of Miguel Angel, your grandfather. He would come watch me paint almost every day. Before I knew it, I was in love."

"Wow, how romantic. So then what happened?"

"We began to meet secretly."

"Why did you have to hide?"

"We were afraid of my mother's disapproval."

"But why?"

"Because he wasn't from a prominent family, and his skin color was a little too olive."

That's weird, I thought to myself. *Sure, they wanted her to marry a good man who could pay for everything. But my skin is pretty olive, too; what difference would that make?* This was the second time I had heard this, and I didn't like it.

As I grew older, I learned that in Latin countries, skin color is very important. The lighter your skin, the more you were liked by everyone and accepted into society. I experience this personally because my oldest sister Nancy was blond with blue eyes, and my oldest brother Charles had big blond curls when he was little. They both took after my father's side. My brother Bobby and I were olive-complexioned, with black hair. One of my father's sisters, a blond-haired woman who lived in Puerto Rico, was well-off. She was married to the mayor of Ponce. They even owned the baseball team. They would send for my siblings Charlie and Nancy during summer vacations. I remember the two would return with tons of toys, dresses, and jewelry; but had been given nothing for Bobby and me.

But back to Mamá's story. She said, "One evening, while I was rocking on the front porch, Miguel Angel came up to me and handed me a beautiful bouquet of roses, and asked me to marry him."

"*Que romantico*," my mother said.

"What did you tell him?" I asked.

"I answered 'Yes!' without any hesitation. The next day at breakfast, I announced to my parents that I was in love with Miguel Angel, and he had asked me to marry him. *Dios mio*, everyone at the breakfast table froze. They were all in shock. You could hear a pin drop. My parents kept their composure and remained quiet.

"After breakfast, my parents went into the library to discuss my future. I was very bold for a sixteen-year-old woman in those days. Anyway, my parents went across the hall into the library, and closed the door. I put my ear next to the door. Even though I was determined to marry your grandfather, I wanted my parents' blessing.

"The conversation went something like this. 'Who is this Miguel Angel?' asked my mother.

"My father responded, 'All I know about him is that he is a hard-working man. I've seen him in the fields.'

"'What is his last name? What family does he come from? How can our Alicia marry such a man? He is not from our class, and he is *muy trigueño*—very dark. Who knows if he has black blood?'

"'I will find out who he is,' my father answered. 'I will speak to Rogelio.'

"I quickly hid as my father went out to the fields to speak to his hiring manager, Rogelio," Mamá continued. "I saw my father pull Rogelio aside and begin to ask him questions. When my father returned, he asked to speak to me in the library. I followed my father in. I had a lump in my throat. My father went behind his desk and sat down as if he were going to start a business meeting. My mother walked in slowly, putting her hand on his left shoulder as she stood behind him. Neither of them was smiling, which made me very nervous.

"My father said to me, '*Por favor*, sit down. Do you really love this man, Miguel Angel?'

"'Yes, Papá,' I responded.

"'I have spoken to Rogelio. He explained that Miguel Angel is the son of Miguel Angel Gongora the elder, a sugar plantation owner from Camagüey who was taken prisoner by the Spaniards during the war. So I asked Rogelio where Miguel Angel's father was now, and why he was working for me. It turns out, his father was taken prisoner, and spent several years in Spain. When he was freed and returned to Cuba, Miguel Angel the elder found his wife remarried."

"'*Dios mío*, how horrible.' I said. 'Imagine coming home and finding this out! Poor Miguel; it's a terrible situation for everyone.'"

"So what did Miguel's mother do?" I asked

"She stayed with her new husband. That's when Miguel the elder decided to sell all he could and went back to Spain; but before he did, he left his sister, Ines, in charge of all his affairs. He instructed his sister Ines to give his land to his son when he turned eighteen and, until then, to provide him with a monthly stipend."

"So what happened to his property and money?" I asked.

"My father said Miguel Angel never got his inheritance. Ines gave everything to her sons. That's why he left Camagüey and came to Sagua la Grande, and started working on my father's plantation."

Then my father said, "Your mother and I have decided to give you our blessings and support you in every way we can."

"Could you imagine how relieved and happy I was? It was the happiest day of my life. I couldn't wait to tell Miguel Angel. Of course, he had to formally ask my father for my hand. My father said to me, 'Ask Miguel to come to dinner on Sunday, after church.'

"I ran up and kissed both of them, and thanked my parents profusely."

My mother had never heard this story, and of course, neither had I. "Mamá, tell us more. And when are you going to tell us about how your mother died?"

"Let's talk tomorrow. I'm tired; I need to rest. *Buenas noches*." Mamá went to bed while my mother and I stayed up a little while longer.

I said to my mother, "I hope she tells us soon. I'm getting impatient."

My mother said, "Don't hurry her. She will tell us when she's ready. I've waited this long; I can wait a little longer."

21

Dr. Castellano

El Morro, Havana

Staying at this cabin and listening to Mamá's stories was perfect, because there was no TV. The next day, after dinner, my mother, my little sisters, and I were all sitting on the front porch, eagerly waiting for Mamá to continue telling her story.

My grandmother sat on the rocking chair and began her story once more. "My parents were very happy with all their ten children and had big plans for all of us. My brothers Nestor, Domingo, Paco, Mario, Hector, Ricardo, and Francisco were all going to be educated in the United States."

"Only the boys?" I asked. "What about the girls?"

"Oh no, girls didn't leave home. We were brought up to marry fine gentlemen. I became, as you know, a teacher, which was very unusual at that time. But getting back to my mother, although she gave me her blessing to marry Miguel Angel, I knew she still felt he wasn't of our class. But she never said anything more regarding his pedigree.

"It was right during this time when I noticed my mother hadn't been feeling well. She had been complaining of terrible pain in her stomach. My father took her to the best doctors of Sagua la Grande, but it seemed they couldn't come up with a diagnosis. The doctors suggested that my father take my mother to Havana to see a specialist.

"My mother planned our trip to Havana, which was about three hours away by train. She asked her sister Elvira, my aunt who lived with us, to take charge of the servants and the children's nannies while we were gone. A nurse and I accompanied my mother on the journey. This was my first trip to Havana. I was very concerned about my mother, but I was also very excited to see Havana. I had heard and read so much about Havana; after all, it is the capital of Cuba.

"My father stayed back to take care of his business. He was in the middle of negotiations. He and his brother-in-law Salvador (my mother's brother, my uncle) had put a bid on a sugar plantation in Camagüey, the province where Miguel Angel was from.

"My mother, the nurse, and I pulled into Havana Central Train Station. I was in awe when I stepped off the train and looked around. In the 1900s, Havana's architecture was mainly Spanish Colonial. The buildings were pristine, with gilded, scrolled-iron gates, tall arches supported by Corinthian columns, and roofs topped by cornices. We were greeted by a cousin, Berta. She was from my mother's side of the family. We stayed with her. I really wanted to stay in a hotel, but it wasn't proper for women to stay in hotels alone.

"The next day, before going to see the doctor, we rode by El Morro, the fifteenth-century Spanish fort. The Cuban flag was flapping in the wind. It had only been two months since it replaced the American flag, and only a year since the Spanish flag has been replaced, which had been there for centuries. I felt very proud knowing that my father and his cousin, General Peraza, were instrumental to Cuba's freedom and the unveiling of the Cuban flag.

"When we arrived at Dr. Castellano's office, my mother was holding her stomach, trying not to complain, but it was obvious she was in a lot of pain. Dr. Castellano showed my mother into his private office, where he would do the examination. The nurse and I sat in the waiting room impatiently. All I could do was worry and think, *What if my mother's illness was severe without a cure? What if she died? What would happen to all my brothers and sisters?* I couldn't bear the thought of losing my dear mother.

"Finally, after what seemed like an eternity, my mother and Dr. Castellano came out. I looked at the doctor's face to see if it was good news, but I couldn't tell. Then I looked at my mother, and because of her upbringing, she was not showing any emotion. But then I looked right into her eyes, and I knew that it was not good news.

"Dr. Castellano sat all three of us down in his parlor and said, 'I'm afraid your illness is serious, and I do not have anything that I can give you that will cure you. The only suggestion I can give you is for you to go to the United States. There's a place in New York called Saratoga Springs. People who have bathed in these waters of the springs have shown very good results. Some people claim that the waters have cured them. Here is the information. Please give Florencio my thanks for the cigars. And please keep me informed of your progress.'

"We all left the office disappointed, but I didn't let my mother notice. I said to her, 'How exciting, a trip to New York!' That seemed to improve everyone's mood.

"The next morning, we caught the train back to Sagua la Grande. When we arrived, my father, Tía Elvira, and all the children were at the station. My mother hugged my father and Tía Elvira, and kissed all my brothers and sisters one by one. My mother tried very hard to hold back her tears, but my father was not fooled, especially when he looked at me. My eyes began to water."

I asked, "So what happened? Did your mother die right after she got home?"

Mamá shook her head no. I looked at my mother. I had never seen my mother like this before. She looked like a scared little girl.

My grandmother said, "I'm so tired, I need to go to bed. *Buenas noches.*" I helped her out of the rocking chair. I felt she couldn't go on because she saw my mother becoming sad. I guess this is why they never talked about it. *You can be sure, as sad as it is, I'm going to find out tomorrow.*

22

La Unión

LEFT: Sunday lunch at La Unión, the plantation house;
ABOVE: The post office at the plantation;
BELOW LEFT: Money that was used at my great-grandfather's plantation;
BELOW: Sugar cane production at La Fe

The next night, we all assembled on the front porch to continue listening to Mamá telling us how her mother died. She began with the continuation of her story about the move from Camagüey to the new sugar plantation.

"They were granted ownership of the plantation, called El Francisco. Both my father and my uncle Santiago were very experienced and It did not take long for them to get their new sugar colony operating."

"What does 'sugar colony' mean?"

"Colonies are privately owned or rented parcels of land used to grow sugarcane. There were several sugar colonies on the plantation. Some were rented out. My father's colony—called La Fe, 'the Faith'— was the largest. They even had their own money. I still have a coin with my father's colony's name on it."

"Could you buy anything with his money?"

"Yes, but only at the plantation. It was like a small town."

(Coincidentally, in 2019 I got a phone call from my cousin Nacho. He told me he had collected three coins from our great-grandfather's colony and asked me, "Would you like one?" "Absolutely," I answered.)

Mamá continued. "The plantation had everything: a school where I taught my first class, a church, even a post office. My father and Tío Santiago were very excited for the family to arrive. My mother, Cerila, along with my brothers and sisters, Tía Elvira, the nannies and servants, and I arrived at La Fe. There were miles and miles of sugarcane. My brothers screamed with excitement when they saw the train. The train came right into El Francisco, carrying the sugar cane that was being shipped.

"Our house was beautiful. It was called La Unión. It was a Spanish Colonial home with ten rooms, including a library and a music room. The house sat on a hill surrounded by beautiful trees and overlooking the sugarcane fields. When my father saw my mother, he put his arms around her, and they embraced. Tears rolled down my mother's face as she said, 'What a magnificent place to raise our family.'

"My father took my mother by the hand and led us to one side of the house. He showed her a very long, stone dining table that sat under a portico with draping lavender bougainvillea. He said proudly to my mother, 'This is where we will have our Sunday lunch. Did you notice the bicycle path? The children are going to love it here.'

"The next morning at breakfast, a servant pulled my father aside and gave him a message from my mother. 'Tell Señor Peraza that I'm not feeling well and won't be down for breakfast.' Very concerned, my father went up to see my mother right away. He walked in and saw her looking pale. He said to her, 'Perhaps the move was too much for you. Do you think you should go to Saratoga springs in the United States? the place Dr. Castellano recommended? I will go with you and take care of you.'

"My mother replied, 'Maybe I should, but you must stay and take care of your new business. I'll take a nurse with me. Could you tell my sister Elvira to come and see me?'

"'Of course,' said my father. 'Elvira, Cerila wants to see you. She is in her room. She is not feeling well.'

"'I will go to her immediately.'

"Elvira knocked and my mother said, 'Enter. Come here, my dear sister, I need to talk to you. I'm not well. I'm going to Saratoga Springs. I'm going take Dr. Castellano's advice. I need you to stay and take care of my children; and if anything should happen to me, I want you to marry Florencio so my children will have a mother.'

"'Please don't speak like that. You are going to get well,' said Elvira.

"'Please promise me that you will do as I say.'

"'Yes, my dear sister, I promise.'

"My father didn't want the children to know that my mother was very ill. He began to show them around. There's also a beautiful river on the east side of the plantation. It's about a thirty-minute walk from the main house. He took them all to the river and told them, 'Do not swim here unless you are accompanied by an adult. But right now, I am here, so enjoy.'

"The older boys tore off their clothes and jumped in. What a happy bunch of kids. My little sister Catita (short for Clara Lisa) and I sat under a tree, enjoying watching my brothers swim.

"After an hour my father said 'Vamos, it's time to get back to the house,' We all headed back to the house, singing and laughing. What happiness! When we arrived at the house, there was a beautiful Arabian horse. Nestor, the oldest of my brothers asked, 'Is this horse for me?'

"My father said, 'No, I don't know who that horse belongs to.'

"When we entered the house, the servant said, 'There is a young gentleman sitting in the library.'"

"Who is it?" I asked.

"'Miguel Angel Gongora,' said the servant.

"It had been six months since I had seen him. On the very day my parents gave him their approval, he had gone to see what he could do about his inheritance. I parted the library's pocket doors in one quick motion. There he was, standing and dressed in an elegant, cream-colored linen suit. We looked at each other, and ran into an embrace.

"I said to him, 'You look like a *señor*, mature and strong. And look at me, I look like a real woman,' as I pulled my hair behind my ears.

"'No, you look even more beautiful than I remember,' said Miguel.

"'Tell me what happened. I want to hear everything,' I said.

"This is what had happened. My father had recommended an attorney to help Miguel Angel. The attorney was magnificent. Although Miguel didn't get his father's property, he got a handsome settlement, and was going to buy a cattle ranch. He said he wanted to give me the life I was accustomed to. Now that he was established, we could get married.

"I couldn't believe this was really happening. I was so happy, and then I got really sad because I was so worried about my mother. I called my father so that Miguel could give him the good news himself. After Miguel told him, he asked my father for my hand. It was perfect. He now had plenty of money to go into his own business.

"My father gave his permission for us to be married, and I ran up the stairs to tell my mother. I knocked very softly on her door; I didn't want to disturb her. My mother asked, 'Who's there?'

"'*Soy yo Alicia.*'

"'*Entre.*'

"'Mamá, Papá has given me permission to marry Miguel. He received most of the money that was owed to him.'

"'*Que bueno, felicidades, mija,*' my mother answered in a weak voice. 'We must plan your wedding. I will go to the United States after the wedding.' I had never felt so happy," said Mamá.

"Mamá, did you have a big wedding?" I asked.

"No, it was a simple wedding. We got married in the little chapel on the plantation. And after the wedding, we went back to the house and drank champagne and ate cake. I wore a beautiful white dress with lace that Tía Elvira made, and I wore a fine white mantilla that came from Spain."

"How beautiful," I said. "Mamá, what happened to the plantation? Who lives there now?"

Mamá answered, "No one from our family. My father left the plantation to me and your grandfather, and to my brother Nestor and his wife. My brother sold the plantation and bought a mansion in Havana. I never received my inheritance."

I asked, "But why?"

"At the time, your grandfather and I were doing very well with our cattle ranch, so I never asked my brother for my part of the money, and he never offered it to me. I figured I'd get it someday. But unfortunately, the day came when I really needed the money; and I asked him for it. His response was 'I'm sorry, my sister, it's all gone.' There was nothing left to do. I should have gotten my money at the time of the plantation was sold."

23

The Beginning and the End

My great-grandparents Cerila and Florencio

Mama continued her story, "Shortly after my wedding, my mother left for Saratoga Springs. It was a very long trip. She had to go to Havana to catch the boat. Two weeks later we received a telegram from my mother's nurse, saying 'I regret to tell you that Señora Peraza died this morning at 10 A.M. from pneumonia.' It's still a mystery what was causing her pain that led her to Saratoga Springs.

"It was horrible. I couldn't believe my ears. My dear mother died and left us all behind. She was so young."

We all had tears rolling down our faces, especially my mother.

"How old was she?" I asked.

"She was only forty-two years old."

"Mamá, what did your father do?"

"He had her body shipped back to Cuba. You can't imagine how much I dreaded seeing my mother's coffin. I couldn't bear it. It was too much for me. All I could think of was my beautiful loving mother locked in a box with no air. Just the thought of it terrified me. But I had to be strong for my little brothers and sisters.

"They brought the coffin to our new home, La Unión. We sat for one whole night, just staring at this coffin, with the priest leading us through the rosary over and over. I thought that night would never end. Tía Elvira was so wonderful. She spent time consoling each and every one of us.

"Finally, the morning came. We all went by horse and carriage to what would become our family cemetery. The priest spoke beautifully about what a devoted Catholic, mother, wife, sister, and friend she had been. His words did not fill my emptiness or my grief, but I knew that even with a hole in my heart, I had to look to the future for the sake of my siblings and my new husband. I went every Sunday to her grave and placed her favorite flowers, gardenias, and said a rosary.

"Tía Elvira and my father came to me first to tell me they were getting married. I knew it was my mother's wishes. It was all so strange and all so fast. I had just married your grandfather, then my mother's death, then my father marrying Tía Elvira. I always loved Tía Elvira, but she could never take my mother's place. But it was the best solution for my younger brothers, especially Hector, who was only a year old then. God bless her, she never tried to take my mother's place; she would always be Tía Elvira. As the years passed, we all accepted the situation."

I said to Mamá, "So your father was married to two sisters?"

"Yes. Back in the old days, that's what people did. The important thing was that the children grow up with a mother. It could only be someone who could be trusted and who truly wanted to raise the children. My younger brothers don't remember my mother. Although Tía Elvira became their mother, they always called her 'Tía Elvira.' I also helped with my little brothers until Miguel and I bought Santa Felicita, our beautiful ranch. Santa Felicita was this beautiful three-hundred-acre land ready for us to make it our home. We made it our paradise."

Our vacation came to an end, and so did the mystery of how my great-grandmother died. The next morning, we started packing for the long trip back on the Thruway to Manhattan. I got the directions out and a map to make sure I could reverse the directions. I opened up the map, found Caroga Lake, and noticed we were just a few miles from Saratoga Springs, the place where my great-grandmother had died. How ironic. It was so cathartic for my mother to finally learn about her grandmother's death, and of course, I loved every minute of the trip. The ride home seemed to go a lot faster. I love going away, but it's always great to be back home.

24

Post-Castro Cubans Arrive

My cousin
Magaly and me,
Christmas 2019

When Castro came to power, all of my family members were on board with the new regime at first. As Castro's true colors began to reveal themselves, most of my family, disillusioned, became anti-Castro, except for my cousin Alicia Elena and her family, who still lived in Cuba.

In 1965, Castro announced he was opening the borders, and anyone who wanted to leave the island could leave on boats through the port of Camarioca. Within days, the port was filled with over 3,000 leisure boats that belonged to Cuban exiles in Miami, ready to captain their relatives back to the United States. You could just imagine the frenzy.

Castro immediately put a stop to the flotilla. Instead, he commissioned Cuban ships and flights to transport over 265,000 people. They were called Freedom Flights. My cousin Magaly and her husband Jorge came on one of those flights with their four children. They left behind their beautiful home and swimming pool in El Vedado, along with their three beloved Doberman Pinschers. El Vedado was one of the most desirable neighborhoods in Havana.

I was thirteen years old at the time; I remember feeling so excited at their arrival. I couldn't wait to meet my new cousins. They arrived in Miami with only three changes of clothing, no jewelry, no nothing. They stayed in Hialeah, Florida, with our aunt Elba and uncle Glenn for a few days before coming to New York.

All of my aunts, cousins, and I waited for their arrival at Mamá's apartment on Nagle Avenue. All my new little cousins arrived wearing these lime-green hooded snowsuits. I had never seen such unusual coats before. They were given to them at the Refugee Center in Miami, and I never saw them wearing them again. I also noticed that Magaly was wearing her diamond wedding rings. I wondered how she was able to get her rings out of Cuba, so I asked her.

She answered, "I went to my doctor, who had been a family friend for years. He wrapped my rings in cotton and gave me something to make it easy to swallow them. When I arrived in Hialeah, at Tía Elba's house, I went to the bathroom and retrieved my rings." From that day on, we became favorite cousins, and we still are.

I was amazed at how quickly Jorge found a job, rented an apartment, enrolled his four kids at St. Rose's Catholic private school, and very soon after, started his own business making plastic furniture covers. In the 1960s, plastic furniture covers were all the rage. Jorge became the Henry Ford of the plastic furniture cover industry. He got his customers by knocking from door to door. Once he took their orders, he would measure the furniture, give Magaly the measurements, and she would cut out the plastic. His son Jorgito would then sew the pieces together, and Jorge would then fit the covers on the client's furniture. The plastic covers fit like a glove and gave the furniture a new lease on life.

My mother was one of his first customers. We sat on the clear, gold-tone plastic covers for years. A friend once came to my house and asked, "When are you going to unwrap the furniture? Christmas is over." Jorge quickly built up a reputation, and with that came success and a Tudor home in Whitestone, Queens.

25

Sofrito at 523

523 West 187th Street in Manhattan

In the early 1960s, 523 West 187th Street changed. It was no longer just Jewish and Irish with a sprinkling of everything else. It now had a healthy serving of Cuban. Whenever I walked into my building, I could tell by the aroma who was cooking what, especially the delicious smell of sofrito—the sauce of fried onions, peppers, garlic, and herbs—that was coming from my mother's kitchen. But now, that familiar smell was coming from almost every floor. I was in heaven. I always enjoyed the aromas from all the different nationalities; I was often treated to a lot of delicious meals from all over the world.

I instantly loved all my new Cuban neighbors and had a desire to help them. So at the age of twelve, I appointed myself their ambassador. There were seven new Cuban families in total. All were somehow related to each other. The Gonzalez family arrived first. Then their aunt and uncle, Maruca and Jose, moved in. Little by little, they kept coming. With my broken Spanish, I was determined to help them in any way I could. I would accompany them to doctor appointments, the phone company, Con Edison, and so on; and eventually even became their English teacher. They were all educated professionals or had a trained skill, but had limited English. Some of them had been doctors, schoolteachers, carpenters, lawyers, and bakers. We even had an interior designer, Marta Mendoza. Marta helped make all their apartments look like they had been living there for years, and I loved helping her.

Marta and her husband, Andres, with their little son Andrecito, moved right next door to us. My mother and Marta became close friends, a friendship that would last for the rest of their lives. Our family and the Mendozas moved to Miami around the same time, in the early seventies. Our families are still close to this day. They were all hardworking people who never complained about what they lost. They were just happy to be in the United States, free from Castro's oppression.

Our neighbor Betty Thomashkin, from apartment 2E, whose first husband was Cuban and who had an affection for Cubans, gave me a whole bunch of clothes to give to our neww Cuban neighbors. Among the clothes was an old mink stole. I knew exactly who I was going to give the stole to: Mirella, a young and very pretty woman who must have been in her early thirties. I just knew she would love it. Mirella lived in apartment 6F, the apartment where my parents met and where I was born.

I knocked on Mirella's door, excited to give her my treasure, but I knew I had to be patient and give it to her at the right moment. I didn't want to hurt her feelings; I knew that the Cubans who came here with nothing still carried their pride, and didn't like feeling diminished by handouts.

Mirella opened the door and asked me to sit down, then offered me some Cuban coffee. I could see her discreetly looking at my shopping bag. She handed me the little cup, and I said, *"Gracias."* I said to Mirella that my friend Betty Thomashkin from apartment 2E gave me this mink stole to give to someone, and I thought of you. I pulled it out of the shopping bag very slowly, and gave it to Mirella.

I could see her eyes widen with excitement. She screamed and wrapped the mink stole around her shoulders, looked at herself in the mirror, grabbed wsome bobby pins to put her hair up, and began to stroll around the living room like she had just won the Miss America title.

"I'm glad you are so happy," I said to Mirella. "You really like the mink, and you look really pretty in it."

She answered with a bittersweet smile, "We had so much in Cuba, and we had to leave it all behind. That criminal Castro took everything we owned. I will never have what I had in Cuba, but now I have freedom."

26

The Mariel Boatlift

Mariel Boat Lift, Key West, Florida

In 1980, during the Carter presidency, Castro opened his country's doors and let over 20,000 people go to the United States. What Castro didn't mention was that among them were many undesirables from his jails and insane asylums. When it became apparent this was another of Castro's manipulations, the United States stopped Cubans from entering, including some Cubans who were let out for religious freedom.

On one of those boats were my cousin Cachita, her husband, and their five children. They were able to leave because they were Jehovah's Witnesses. My father and Tía Elba drove to Key West to pick them up. My mother stayed home to prepare a feast. It was an emotional reunion. Everyone cried and hugged each other. Chachita and her family stayed with my parents for three months. As most Cuban exiles did, they quickly got on their feet, found jobs and rented a house.

The Mariel Boatlift was the last opportunity for Cubans to come to the United States. This led Cubans to take desperate measures. Cubans were now risking their lives on man-made rafts. Remember Elian Gonzalez? His mother drowned trying to provide him with a life of freedom. Like her, many have lost their lives. The "wet foot, dry foot" policy accepted Cubans if they were able to put one foot on United States soil. If they were caught before landing, they were sent back to Cuba to face criminal charges for trying to leave.

In 2015, President Obama began negotiations with Cuba. During this time, once again multiple flights from Cuba left for the United States daily. More than a million Cubans emigrated to the United States, leaving behind their homes, possessions, and worst of all, their families. So many lives were lost. What was it all for? Now American capitalism is seeping into Cuba, little by little. My only hope is that the Cuban people there benefit from new opportunities. When Donald Trump was elected president, he quickly undid everything that Obama had changed. Trump stopped tourism from the United States to Cuba, and all passenger vessels and corporate and private flights. Once again, only Cubans and Cuban Americans are allowed to travel to Cuba, via commercial flights.

27

Beautiful Lace Handkerchiefs

Mamá, on her eightieth birthday

In 1968, I was now a young man of sixteen. This was when my afternoon trips down Snake Hill to see Mamá suddenly ended. There would be no more afternoon snacks, no more stories about the pictures in the hall. My dear Mamá was now 83 years old and getting very frail. Mamá had fallen and broken her hip, and my visits were now to Fordham hospital. My mother and all of my aunts, siblings, and cousins visited often as well. It seemed like Mamá was there forever. Mamá was in the hospital for over three months, getting thinner and thinner, until she was released. Going back to her third-floor walk-up apartment on Nagle Avenue would be difficult for her. So all of my aunts came to an agreement to send Mamá to Florida, because Tía Elba and Tío Glenn lived in Hialeah, Florida, in a house with a backyard. It would be easier for Mamá to get around, since there were no steps. My mother was the only one of Mamá's daughters who disagreed. My mother cried and said, "How can you uproot Mamá at her age? It's too much of a change to separate her from all her things, and from all of us. Please don't send her there."

My aunts had their minds made up. Mamá was moving to Florida. *"No aye remedio*—there's no other option," said Tiana.

Tiana took Mamá directly from the hospital to Hialeah. Once again Mamá had no choice but to leave her home. She never went back to her Nagle Avenue apartment.

Christmas was just a few weeks away. This would be the first Nochebuena without Mamá. Tiana went to Florida for Christmas to be with Mamá. I bought a box of fancy ladies' handkerchiefs and wrapped it in Christmas paper and gave it to my aunt to give to Mamá. On Christmas Eve, my mother called Mamá. When Mamá got on the phone, she said to my mother, "Please send for me. I don't want to die here. I would settle to sleep on your couch."

My mother answered, "I promise I'll send for you."

I asked to speak to my grandmother. "Hello, Mamá, how are you doing?"

She said, "I'm very unhappy. I miss you. Thank you for the beautiful lace handkerchiefs."

"You're welcome. Christmas won't be the same without you, I hope to see you very soon."

That was the last time I ever spoke to Mamá. Right after New Year's, Mama's health went downhill. My mother and my sister Nancy flew down to Florida to be with her. I begged to go but it was unaffordable, so I stayed back to help take care of my younger sisters. When my mother and Nancy arrived in Florida, they went straight to the hospital. When they got there, they found that Mamá could barely speak. Mamá was dying. On January 10, 1969, at the age of eighty-four, Mamá, Alicia María de la Caridad Peraza, took her last breath. Tiana told me later that when she gave Mamá the box of handkerchiefs and told her it was from me, Mamá hugged the box and cried, and said, *"Mijo."*

I feel comfort in knowing that Mamá's original plans for her family to come to New York all came to fruition. Although none of her daughters married Cuban aristocrats, they all found husbands.

My aunt Lila and my uncle Carlos remained in Ecuador, and were well off as Carlos had promised. They went on to have four beautiful children. Lila is the only aunt I didn't get to know very well, as I only met her twice. She was the prettiest of all my aunts. Sadly, in 1994, after forty years of marriage, Carlos Duran left my aunt for their maid, who was thirty years his junior.

Tía Lila died shortly after from a broken heart. I am glad Mamá didn't live to witness the pain that Lila had to endure. Tía Elba's marriage to Tío Glenn wasn't exactly a happy one, nor an unhappy one. They lived comfortably with their two sons in one of the many duplexes he owned.

Tía Elba had a heart of gold. She continued to help all the family in every way she could, including sewing dresses for all the important occasions for the generations that followed, until brain cancer took her in 1983. I and all the family will always miss her beautiful, generous spirit.

When Mamá went to Florida, the marriage between Tiana and Tío Juan Enrique was already in trouble. Mamá and Juan Enrique never got along. There was always upheaval, which created a very tense household. He started coming home late and drunk, and he blamed my grandmother for his bad behavior. When Mamá moved to Florida, my aunt hoped that living alone with her husband and without Mamá would give their marriage a chance. Unfortunately, Tiana's marriage ended anyway. Juan Enrique stayed for another few months. The situation was hopeless. He was coming home later and later, and drunker and drunker, until she found evidence of another woman. That was the end. They were divorced soon after.

After the divorce Tiana gave up the Nagle Avenue apartment and moved to Florida, right next door to Tía Elba and Tío Glenn. It was a new start for her. She decorated her home beautifully, and hung all of Mama's pictures from the Nagle Avenue apartment on the walls of her new home. Tiana eventually developed Alzheimer's, and died when she was almost eighty years old. I remained close to Tiana till the end of her life, and since she had no children of her own, she left me all of Mama's pictures. I now have Mama's paintings with the Cuban palm trees and the family pictures hanging on a wall in my home. I cherish them with all my heart.

My parents stayed married through thick and thin until my father's death. My father died in 1992 with all his children around him including Lillian. My parent's later years were mostly happy and without incident. It's clear to me they loved each other very much. After my father died, my mother remained alone in Florida. All seven of us kids were now married and/or living in other states. I was living in New York and very concerned about my mother living alone and unable to drive. With a lot of persuasion and many phone calls, I convinced my mother to go to the senior citizen center. After her first trip to the center, she called me went she got home.

"How did it go, Mom?" I asked

She answered, "It was great! I met a lot of nice Cuban people my age. In fact, I invited a few of them for dinner tomorrow."

"Wow, that's wonderful," I said.

The dinners continued until the day she called me and said, "I'm getting married to one of the men from the senior citizen center. His name is Angel Borges. He's exactly my age and he is from Camagüey, my home town in Cuba. He was one of the waiters from the hotel where I celebrated my quinces. Isn't that something?"

"Mommy, you don't know this guy, what's the rush?"

"He's a decent, clean man, and he has a car. Besides, I'm Catholic, and I wouldn't want to tarnish you father's memory by just having him move in with me. You know neighbors will talk."

After I hung up, I called all my siblings with the news. Everyone thought my mother had lost her mind making such a rash decision. I also called my cousin Norman, and asked him to prepare a prenuptial agreement. I called my mother back and told her about the prenup; she agreed.

As soon as the document was ready, my mother presented the prenup to Angel. He signed it without hesitation. A couple of years later, we found out that Angel had plenty of money of his own and never asked my mother to sign a prenup. Angel is a very decent, honest man, whom we all grew to like. Of all the siblings, my sister Nancy and I became the closest to Angel. It became clear how much Angel worshipped my mother. Angel was very good to my mother; he always tried to accommodate her in every way.

In 1999 my mother decided to move to Houston, where three of her children were now living—my sisters Denise and Darlene, and me. Her marriage to Angel was fine, but she intuitively knew there was something wrong with her health. When she arrived in Houston, I noticed something was wrong with my mother's memory. I took her to a neurologist. The doctor diagnosed her with early onset Alzheimer's. He prescribed a new pill called Aricept. She took the pill for the rest of her life, and thank God this pill slowed the progress of this disease. In 2012, at the age of 86, after a bad fall, my mother went to live with my sister Nancy in Florida. A couple of years prior to her move, my mother said, "I want to be buried with your father. He was the love of my life."

I said to her, "But Mom, Angel paid for all the final arrangements for the two of you"

"I know, I feel bad about that, but I really want to be buried with your father. He was the father of all my children and my husband of forty-seven years."

"Ok Mom, I'll see what I can do."

My father had been buried in Our Lady of Mercy Catholic Cemetery, near the outskirts of Miami. On my way to his funeral in the limousine along with all my siblings, the driver said to us, "Do you know who's buried here?"

We answered, "No."

"Jackie Gleason."

It made us all laugh because Jackie Gleason was my father's favorite comedian, whom he imitated all through our lives.

Now I went to the cemetery to ask if I could buy the plot adjacent to where my father was buried. They told me there was nothing available. The only thing they could do, they explained, was to move my father to another part of the cemetery, where there were two plots adjacent to each other. The cost to do this was $6,000. I consulted my siblings, and everyone was in agreement and wanted to honor my mother's wishes.

On May 2, 2012, my loving mother and my best friend took her last breath with all of her seven children there. My parents are buried in Our Lady of Mercy Catholic Cemetery, resting side by side, just as my mother wished.

28

Cuba 1993

Trudy and me having lunch at Varadero Beach, Cuba

After Castro's takeover, the United States government largely prohibited travel to Cuba. In 1993, however, Cuban and Cuban American residents were allowed to return to the island to visit family members. This change was not highly publicized. I found out about it purely by coincidence. The Internet still wasn't mainstream. There was a very small article in *The New York Times*. There were restrictions on who was allowed to visit. You had to be either born in Cuba, or a child of an immigrant from Cuba to the United States.

Most post-Castro Cubans were not interested in going back to visit. Some Cubans, because they didn't want to contribute to Castro's economy, and others because they were afraid that Castro would retain them. Cuba considers all Cubans and their descendants to be Cuban citizens. Aside from being gay, I felt very comfortable traveling to

Cuba, because my mother and most of my family came before Castro's revolution.

Visiting Cuba was no longer going to be a vignette dancing in my head. It became a reality, *I'm going to Cuba!* The excitement I felt was euphoric. All I could think about was all those places Mamá and my mother had spoken of. I was now almost forty-two years old. That's a lot of years of dreaming of Cuba. So I called the travel agency that had the ad in *The New York Times,* and asked if I could book a trip to Cuba. They told me to come in. *Oh my God, is this real?*

As a Cuban American citizen, I was allowed to bring a wife or a fiancée. I called my very close friend Trudy, and asked her if she would be interested in going to Cuba with me. Trudy and I met in 1990 in Provincetown, Massachusetts. When Trudy and I met, we looked at each other and right then and there we felt and became instant family.

At the time, Trudy was in a relationship with a woman named Kelly, with whom I also became friends. On one of those beautiful Provincetown summer sunset evenings, while Trudy, Kelly, and I sipped Beautifuls (a blend of cognac and Grand Marnier orange liqueur), they turned to me and said, "We are planning on having a baby, would you be interested in being the father, as the sperm donor?"

In those days, it was really unusual for gay people to have children. I was flattered and told them that I needed a little time to think about it. I come from a large family with tons of nephews and nieces. I always assumed I would have kids. I thought to myself, maybe this was the time.

The next day, I met with them and told them *yes.* All of us were so excited. Unfortunately, Kelly and Trudy's relationship ended shortly thereafter. Nevertheless, Trudy and I remained committed to having a baby.

I introduced Trudy to my entire family. My mother loved Trudy and was ecstatic with the idea of having a grandchild from us. It was perfect that Trudy was going to Cuba with me for many reasons. For one, the fun we were going to have and the prospect of sharing the experience with our child. And there was another reason. For Cuban residents, being gay was against the law. If the government suspected you of being gay, you were sent to hard labor in the fields, or you were sent to jail. Even worse, if you protested your sentence, you were tortured and/or murdered. I assumed the law for a gay visitor might be the same. Not taking any chances, I kept my sexuality a secret. I certainly didn't want any trouble with the Cuban government for my Cuban family, whom I had never met. It was ideal that Trudy and I could go together. We were really close friends, and as far as Cuba was concerned, we looked like a good old-fashioned couple.

Really excited and nervous, I went to the travel agency. They said that I had to apply for a special visa and give a good reason why I wanted to visit Cuba. I applied for the visa for Trudy and myself. By this time, both my aunt Silvia and my uncle Mario had passed, but my uncle Pancho was still alive. He was now ninety-one years old; at least one of my old uncles was still there.

The day I opened the mail to find our passports and our visas felt unbelievable! I immediately called Trudy with the news. I went straight to the travel agency and bought our tickets to Havana. The package included a hotel room, some meals, and airfare from Miami to Jose Martí International Airport in Havana.

29

Controversial Paradise

El Hotel Capri,
Havana, Cuba

On a winter day in February of 1993, Trudy and I flew from New York to Miami. We spent the night at my mother's house in Homestead. The next morning, we got up at 3 A.M. for our 10 A.M. flight to Havana. We arrived at the airport at 5 A.M. to check in. In 1993 there were no metal detectors or scanning machines as of yet. The line with Cubans and Cuban-Americans like myself waiting to be searched was very long. Airport security wanted to ensure we weren't caring any weapons, for fear of hijackers. They searched our luggage and our bodies thoroughly. The baggage weight limit was very strict. If your suitcase was over the limit, they would have you remove items until it was exactly within the weight limit. I'll never forget this one lady on the line. She knew the Cuban system well. She wore several dresses, one on top of the other. I'm sure she wore layers of underclothing too. Her dress was covered with all kinds of decorative pins and safety pins with earrings hanging from them, and five hats stacked one on top of the other on her head. What she wore did not count in the allowed weight limit. She must have been wearing at least an extra hundred pounds.

The flight took only thirty-five minutes from Miami to Havana. No sooner had we gone up in the air, than we were heading back down again. As the people on the plane spotted Havana, they simultaneously began to applaud. Trudy and I looked at each other, laughed, and applauded too. My heart began to pound, while my thoughts raced thinking about what I was about to experience. I was about to land in this controversial paradise.

We got off the plane and proceeded through customs. Suddenly, I felt afraid. There were lots of soldiers dressed in their deep-green uniforms, holding machine guns and standing everywhere you looked. We proceeded to a line to pay the required airport tax, which for the two of us totaled $10.

I slipped a $20 bill to a lady who sat behind window with bars.

She said, *"Gracias."*

"Mi cambió, por favor." I asked her for my change.

She stared at me and said, "What change?"

I said, "Never mind," and walked away from the window. I said to Trudy, "We really need to be careful. People here are desperate."

We got on the bus to the hotel. I couldn't believe my eyes. There were hundreds of people on old dilapidated bicycles wearing worn-out clothes. As we started going through the streets, you could see the old Spanish Colonial buildings falling apart and ready to crumble. When I looked at the cars, it was like being in a time warp. All the cars were from the 1950s and still running. They kept them together with tin cans and strings. You could tell these Cubans had become very resourceful. It was all about survival. My excitement quickly turned into sadness. This was Cuba now, not the Cuba that Mamá knew. I'm sort of glad she never had to witness what had become of her beloved Cuba.

30

Havana

Havana

We arrived at El Hotel Capri, the hotel that was famous for its pool on the roof. You got the impression that the hotel had been something in its heyday, but those days were long gone. The hotel had fallen into severe disrepair.

The room had twin beds with really skinny mattresses and sheets with holes. There was a black-and-white TV sitting on an old dresser. I turned the TV on to see what Cuban television was like. The first person who appeared on the screen was Fidel Castro. He was giving a speech to a very enthusiastic crowd. Every time he paused, the crowd would go wild, as if he were a rock star, and yell out *"Viva la revolución!"* When I changed the channel, there he was again. He was on every channel. Trudy and I laughed and said to each other that this program could get really old very quickly.

We showered (oh yeah, four drops of water came out), got dressed, and went down for dinner. I had heard that there was a scarcity of food, but whatever we were going to be served was Cuban, and I really love Cuban food. How bad could it be? Well, we got on a buffet line and started to put these unrecognizable items on our plate. The fruit was the only thing that was edible. The rest had no taste and was totally dry. This was not Cuban food. This was sad food.

The next morning, it was the same buffet. I said to Trudy, "I'm going to lose a few pounds on this trip." Trudy suggested going sightseeing, so off we went. Just one block away was the famous Hotel Nacional. It was in pristine condition inside and out, with beautiful gardens overlooking the harbor. We went through a long, arched hallway before we got to the bar. As soon as you entered the bar you were greeted by a bronze bust of Nat King Cole sitting on a pedestal. He was beloved by all Cubans. Nat recorded several albums, all in Spanish, right in Havana. He was a regular at The Tropicana. We found two seats at the bar and ordered a couple of Cuba Libres or Mentiritas. It was like we were back in the fifties.

The back of the Hotel Nacional faces the Malecón, a sea wall in Havana's harbor where lovers stroll. Trudy and I walking down the Malecón and enjoyed the sight of the waves crashing right against it. In the distance we saw El Morro, the Spanish fortress that was built in the beginning of the sixteenth century. The Cuban flag was flapping in the wind. I imagined El Morro looked just like the way Mamá saw it on her first trip to Havana in 1906.

After we got back to the hotel, I suggested we go to Coppelia, the famous ice cream parlor where gay men meet secretly. It was in the movie *Fresa y Chocolate* (*Strawberry and Chocolate*), one of the first movies to come out of communist Cuba. Coppelia was only a couple of blocks from our hotel. We went and sat on the outdoor porch and ordered strawberry and chocolate ice cream, just as in the movie. Trudy and I looked around to see if we could pick out a gay couple having a secret ice cream rendezvous. I'm pretty sure we did. It made me sad to think that homosexuals had to live in fear for their lives if they were found out. So much for Cuba Libre!

After we had ice cream, we decided to take a walk through old Havana. It was really sad to see all those beautiful iconic buildings falling apart. But it was still charming in a surreal way. We went into a deteriorating hotel. There was this old man who was hand-rolling cigars in the lobby. You could tell by his expertise that he had been rolling cigars for years. I bought a few cigars from him, and I lit one right there. The smell alone was amazing. It tasted completely different from any cigar I had ever smoked. The flavor was deep, earthy, and smooth. I smoked cigars every day while I was there. I even managed to smuggle a few back to the United States.

We didn't want to spend too much time in Havana because I wanted to go to Las Tunas, which is in Santiago, the province where Teddy Roosevelt marched up San Juan Hill and defeated the Spaniards in the Spanish-American War. Santiago is the most eastern province in Cuba, where my Tío Pancho and my remaining cousins, whom I had never met, still lived. But before we left Havana, there was one more place I had to see: The Tropicana, the Cuban cathedral of nightclubs.

I had first heard about the Tropicana at this little Cuban bar in New York called the Tijuana Cat. It was on West 46th Street, on restaurant row, the place where I got my first singing job. I was hired with the help of a friend Musme, a child star from Havana who was a Cuban Chinese female impersonator who sang in a falsetto soprano voice. He was amazing and funny, too. He was the Saturday-night headliner. There were many other famous Cuban stars who performed there. The Tijuana Cat was a haven for famous exiled Cuban artists. I met so many incredible Cuban artists including Celia Cruz, Olga y Tony, and Leonela Gonzalez, who was the model for the Tropicana logo. My friend Musme, from Washington Heights, heard me sing, and said that he was going to speak to the owner, Pepe. At the time, I was twenty-two years old with a repertoire that consisted of two songs in Spanish, *Nosotros* and *Amor*, songs I heard on my mother's Eydie Gormé and Los Panchos Trio album of Spanish love songs. Musme talked me up to the owner. Pepe hired me for three consecutive Friday nights, and if it went well, he would extend my contract. With my limited Spanish, I rehearsed with the house pianist, Juan Pires, who helped me with my new Spanish repertoire. I was a success. I continued working there for the next three years, until the Tijuana Cat closed. Meeting all these Cuban performers inspired me and increased my desire to someday visit the Tropicana nightclub in Cuba.

Trudy and I got dressed in our nightclub attire, hailed a taxi, and went to the Tropicana. When we arrived, the doorman, who was dressed in a very fancy uniform, opened our door. I gave him a dollar tip. He thanked me as if I had handed him a hundred-dollar bill. I asked him, "How long have you been working here?"

He answered, "Since the day they opened the door." He had been the Tropicana doorman for over fifty years.

We went in, and saw that there were two rooms for shows. On the right was the famous room with the retractable glass roof. We were escorted to the room on the left that led to a big outdoor area with long tables, one huge stage, and other small stages, all set within enormous banyan trees. We were seated.

The show began, the lights starting to illuminate different stages at different times. The bongos and timbales were beating away, getting louder and louder into a frenzy of rhythms. It was so exciting to sit at a table and listen to real Afro-Cuban music.

Then a parade of sexy, voluptuous, almost naked, mocha-colored women, while balancing very tall, elaborate headdresses, started shaking to the pulse of the drums. Wow! Now THIS is Cuba.

After the incredible show, the audience was invited to dance on the stage. Of course I was not going to miss this opportunity. Trudy and I rumbaed the night away.

There was still one more thing I wanted to see before we went to see my family: Varadero Beach, the most famous beach in all of Cuba. The next morning, we bought round-trip bus tickets to Varadero. Halfway there, the bus stopped at the most breathtaking spot I had ever seen, just before we crossed the Bacunayaagua Bridge in Matanzas. Below the bridge was a winding river, and across were mountains and mountains covered with thousands of palm trees. I had never seen anything like it. It was magnificent.

We got back into the bus and continued on to Varadero. We arrived to see a blazing sun shining over crystal-clear turquoise waters, and sand as white and fine as sugar. The beach had just reopened for tourists only, after being closed for over forty years. We changed into our bathing suits and walked down the beach. The sand was so soft, it tickled as it slipped through our toes. We waded into the warm soothing ocean. It seemed like you could walk forever without the water getting deep.

After our swim, we went into the restaurant and sat down at a table facing the ocean. We were the only customers that day. It was sad to see what was one of Cuba's hotspots totally deserted. We ordered some fried fish and Cuba Libres. We pretended it was during Cuba's heyday and had a ball. Now I can say that I swam in one of the world's most beautiful beaches, Varadero.

31

Las Tunas

Me with Cuban cousins in Las Tunas, Cuba

The next morning, we went back to the airport to catch a flight to Holguín, Santiago, the closest airport to Las Tunas, where my family lived.

As we were approaching Holguín, I said to Trudy, "How am I going to recognize my cousins, and how are they going to recognize me?" None of us had ever met before. The only person I had met was my ninety-one-year-old Tío Pancho, but the last time I saw him was in 1958, when I was six years old.

When we got on the plane, it was filled with condensation; you couldn't see in front of you. I'm not fond of flying. Nervously, I said to Trudy, "I hope this old plane makes it."

Thank God we landed safely. We deplaned, got our luggage, and went out onto this roof that overlooked the cars and the people below.

I peered over the wall, and I heard a whole bunch of people yelling out *"Roni! Roni!"*—my name in Spanish. I smiled and waved to them. Trudy and I went downstairs and started hugging my cousins as if we had known each other our whole lives. I introduced Trudy to all of them as they said their names. We met my cousins Eduardo and Alicia, who were my uncle Mario's children. The moment I saw Eduardo, it became clear to me how they had recognized me. We looked like brothers. We even had the same crooked nose. We laughed when we realized it.

There were more cousins and second cousins, along with wives and husbands. It would take me a long time before I memorized all their names. The younger generation had nontraditional names, like Milady, Martna, and Yonise.

They said, "Come with me." I assumed we were going to some kind of vehicle, a bus or a car, but no, it was a horse and buggy. None of them owned a car. They had borrowed the horse and buggy from a friend who lived in the country. It was literally like going back in time. They were apologetic and a little embarrassed. I was overjoyed; do you know how much this would cost in Central Park?

It was so much fun riding while getting to know them. We arrived at my cousin Alicia's house. It might get confusing as there are five Alicias in my family, including Mamá. The house was owned originally by my uncle Mario, their father. I had never gotten to meet Tío Mario. I almost met him in 1983, because as an elder he received permission to come to United States. Unfortunately, at the airport, while he was getting ready to board the plane, a government official stopped him. They revoked his visa on the spot and sent him home without explanation. It was a devastating disappointment for everyone. My mother remembered his favorite food and spent the day preparing everything for his arrival. All of my aunts, cousins were there too, awaiting Tío Mario's arrival. Neither my mother nor any of us ever got to see him again. He died the following year.

You could tell Tío Mario's house must have been really nice in its time. It had marble columns in the entryway and Moorish tile through-out, but sadly it was decaying. The bathroom shower didn't work. We washed with a bucket of water. The kitchen went back to the old days, with a stove with just one burner. My cousin Alicia gave us the best room in the house, the master bedroom, which was right off the street.

In the small backyard was a little black animal. I'm not sure if it was a goat, a lamb, or pig. I didn't want to know because my cousin Alicia pointed at it and said, "We saved him to eat while you are here." I thanked her, and I knew it was a big sacrifice for them. Besides, killing an animal in your backyard was against the law. If you got caught, they would send you to jail.

We unpacked and I gave them everything we had brought. They were very grateful. I asked if there were any stores where I could buy food and drinks.

Eduardo said, "They only allow tourists to buy things."

The store was in the hotel gift shop. We went to the hotel, and they didn't let my cousin in. I bought a few things, including Havana Club rum.

When we got back to the house, we had a party with a show. My cousin Alicia came out singing and dancing like a Spanish Gypsy. She was truly wonderful. I felt I was back in Washington Heights at one of my father's house parties. But then two of my younger straight cousins appeared in full drag with dresses, full make-up, and high heels, with their legs as skinny as pencils. Clearly they were making fun. Trudy and I couldn't believe our eyes and laughed while in shock. This would never happen at one of my father's house parties.

32

Tío Pancho

Tío Pancho
and me.

The next day, we all got up nice and early and went shopping at the hotel gift shop. This time, there were about ten cousins with Trudy and me. I allotted each of them $100 to shop. The catch was I had to go in the hotel gift shop with each one of them, one at a time. We spent the whole day there. By the end, we were all tired and very happy with the items and food that they hadn't had in years.

On the way home, we were all exhausted and hungry. My cousins told me that there was a little restaurant in a nearby hotel, and with permission they might let us all in. I went in and asked the man for permission to bring my cousins in for dinner. Permission was needed because locals were not allowed inside the hotels or in restaurants.

Imagine not having the freedom to be able to do something as simple as that. The manager said yes and took us to a private dining room way in the back where no one could see us. My cousins had not been in a restaurant since 1959, since Castro came to power. We all ate and drank Cuban rum to our hearts' content. We laughed and sang all the way back to the house.

The next day my cousin Eduardo took us to the center of the town. The town of Las Tunas was small but charming. It was built during Spanish Colonial times. It had the traditional square in the center, with the church right on the square, and a small museum on the opposite side. We all walked around the square and meandered into the museum.

My cousin Eduardo said, "Look over here."

Behind a big glass case, which looked like it belonged in a department store, was a collection of native Indian artifacts dating back to Columbus's time. There were tools, arrowheads, and eating utensils. At the bottom of the glass case, there was a sign in Spanish that read, "The contents of the display were donated by Alicia Peraza." It was Mamá, my grandmother. That was a great moment.

I still hadn't seen my old uncle Pancho, who also lived in La Tunas. I asked my cousin Eduardo, "Where does he live?"

He said, "I'll take you to see him tomorrow."

The next day, Trudy, my cousin Eduardo, and I went to visit my uncle. I asked Eduardo, "Why aren't the others coming?"

He said, "We don't visit him because his granddaughter Silvita lives with him."

"And why not?"

"Because Silvita works for the government. She's the *fiscal*, the district attorney. Her job is to put anti-Castro people in jail, and you know we are anti-Castro."

"Oh, I see." *How sad*, I thought to myself. *A government separates families by a sea that's only ninety miles wide, and also families who live only blocks apart.*

Silvita is Alicia Elena's daughter, my blond cousin who was in the photograph with my grandfather Miguel—the photograph Mamá showed me many years ago. I brought some presents that included toilet paper. *This is so weird*, I thought, *giving toilet paper as a gift to cousins we've never met before*. To them, toilet paper was better than chocolate.

We walked through the square to Tío Pancho's house and knocked on the door. This pretty young woman with blond hair opened it.

My cousin Eduardo said to Silvita, pointing to me, "This is your cousin Roni. He is our Aunt Irma's son."

We all kissed hello. It's a Latin custom to kiss all family members on the cheek upon greeting or saying goodbye, even if you have never met before. She invited us to sit in the *recibidor*, a small parlor before the main living room. I looked around, trying not be too obvious. Their house was in much better condition than my other cousin Alicia's house.

I said to Silvita, "What a beautiful house you have."

She answered, "It was decorated by your aunt Silvia, my grandmother, before she died."

In 1982, for the first time, Castro allowed elderly people to visit the United States if they had a connection to the government. If they didn't return, their family would be punished. Tía Silvia's son-in-law, Enrique, was communist and held a high position in Castro's government, so she had no problem leaving. It had been over twenty-five years since Tía Silvia's last visit. It was a bittersweet occasion. She was so happy to see everyone, but lamented not seeing Mamá. Tía Silvia was then in her mid-seventies, and still had the same fun spirit. As a joke, I smelled her hair, just as I did when I was a kid. She and mother both laughed, remembering that's what I did those many years ago. We took her to Radio City Music Hall, just as we had done in 1958. I was so glad I had gotten to see her again. What I didn't know at the time was that it would be the last time I would ever see her. Almost exactly a year later we received a letter from her daughter, saying that Tía Silvia had passed away.

Now, ten years later, I was sitting in Tía Silvia's living room, in Cuba. Her absence made me feel profoundly sad. I wished she would still have been alive so I could have seen her just one more time. As I looked around her pretty house, it was clear to me, this was her house, because there were many souvenirs on her walls from her New York City trips. In addition, there were two of Mamá's paintings hanging on the wall, very similar to the ones Mamá had hanging in her living room on Nagle Avenue. I'm sure Mamá painted them around the same time, when she was a young woman in Sagua La Grande.

Then my old uncle Pancho came out. He gave me a hug, and tears rolled down his face. I looked at him and thought he was so little. I guess that was because I had been six years old the last time I saw him; when you're six, everyone is tall. Tío Pancho had been retired for many years. He had been the president of the Royal Bank of Canada, a job he kept until he retired. Tío Pancho was always very elegant. He was dressed in a starched white *guayabera*, the traditional Cuban shirt. *Guayaberas* are worn out over the pants, and have pockets and fine pleats in the front.

His granddaughter Silvita brought some Cuban coffee on a tray and passed it around. As the five of us sat and drank the coffee, Silvita turned to me and said, "I heard that you sing."

"Yes, and I heard you sing, too."

She said, "If you sing, I will."

So I starting singing *Besame Mucho*. She smiled and said, "How beautiful," and began singing a tango.

What a sweet voice she had. What a moment. We had just met, and now we were singing together as if we had known each other our whole lives.

33

Palm Trees at Santa Felicita

Santa Felicita, my grandparents' cattle ranch, 1993

There were two places I really wanted to see: Santa Felicita, the cattle ranch where my mother spent her childhood; and Camagüey, the town where she last lived in Cuba.

There was no public transportation to go anywhere, let alone to the countryside or to another town. I asked my cousin Eduardo, "How can I see these places?"

He said, "Let me see what I can do." And off he went.

About an hour later, he came back with a big smile. He said, "I've got good news for you. My friend who works for the electric company is going to take us on his company truck tomorrow morning. Can you give him $100?"

I said, "Sure."

How exciting; I was finally going to Santa Felicita, my grandparents' ranch! My mind began to race. All the memories kept flooding in. My mother's childhood, Mamá's old life as she knew it, my grandfather's decision to leave our family, the palm trees, and the house with the long mahogany dining room table.

The next morning, we were eagerly awaiting the arrival of Rafa (short for Rafael), the guy with the truck from the electric company. Rafa pulled up in this old vehicle that looked like the one on the Beverly Hillbillies show. When I saw it, I said to Trudy, "This old jalopy will never make it." Then I said a little prayer to myself: "Please, God, let this old truck get us there!"

Of course, there was no GPS yet, and there weren't any maps. Maps wouldn't do us any good anyway, since there were no signs on the roads. Eduardo was the only one left in the family who knew where Santa Felicita was. After Castro took over, the names of many towns and properties had been changed, among them that of Santa Felicita. Castro had also reconfigured the provinces, breaking them up into smaller territories and renaming some of them as well. Although Eduardo hadn't been to Santa Felicita in many years, he was pretty sure he remembered the way. Eduardo sat in the front directing Rafa to Santa Felicita. The rest of us climbed onto the back of the truck and sat on some metal boxes. None of us cared, all that mattered was that we were going to Santa Felicita.

We started down the street that led out of Las Tunas. Very soon, we were on old dirt roads that had been neglected for years, full of huge potholes. They weren't potholes; they were craters. It was like an obstacle course! We could tell Rafa had experience driving along these dilapidated roads, the way he drove around the potholes with precision. This was very reassuring. We were all so happy, we started singing. We sang old Cuban songs, songs that our parents and grandparents used to sing to us. It was pure joy. We would all yell out *"Aye!"* and laugh every time we turned sharply past a pothole.

All of a sudden, it started to rain, and I mean raindrops that were the size of silver dollars. We had no umbrellas, and this made us laugh even more. Getting drenched didn't stop us from singing.

The truck stopped after about an hour. Eduardo yelled out, "We're here!"

I couldn't believe it. My stomach began to tickle with excitement. My heart started to pound. My whole body was filled with emotion and about to burst. We were finally at the entrance of Santa Felicita.

Just at this moment, like magic, the rain stopped and the sun came out. It was the most magnificent sun I had ever seen. Everything started to shine. The wet trees looked like Christmas trees all lit up. The potholes on the road ahead glistened like little mirrors. Everything was shimmering. The smell of the pure air after the rainfall was divine. I thought I was in Hollywood on the movie set of *The Ten Commandments*, in the scene when Moses parts the Red Sea and the sky transforms from this dark gray into a rainbow of colors. I felt I was personally being welcomed by my ancestors, and by God.

We started down this long road lined with the royal palm trees. I said to Trudy, "The palm trees are still here. These are the palm trees my mother spoke about."

Coming up the road was an old man dragging a horse and wagon loaded with sugarcane. You could tell he worked in the sun all the time. The skin on his face resembled dark-chocolate leather. He looked to be at least a hundred years old. I asked him if he lived here.

Without a change in his expression, he said, "No, I just work here for the government." And continued dragging his cart, not missing a beat.

We continued down the road, and there on the right was the dairy barn where Mamá had made buttercream and cheese. All along the road were old abandoned pieces of wagons and farm tools. They looked like little dead soldiers left over from a war. I wondered if they were from my mother's time. They must have been. They looked really old.

I knew from what my mother had told me that if we continued

straight ahead, we would come to her house, and it would be on the left. I looked all around. There was no house, no porch, no dining room table.

I asked my cousin Eduardo, "What happened to our grandparents' house?"

He said with a shrug, "The government. They let it go, just like everything else."

My heart sank. I had been so looking forward to going into Mamá's house. I wanted to go inside and walk through all the rooms. I wanted to feel what it had felt like to be there. I looked around again, still hoping to see something of the remains. But I realized it was completely gone, because I was standing in the right place: on the cement foundations.

I started to walk, imagining where the rooms had been. I stood on the spot where I thought the dining room table must have been, thinking this was where they had had all those great meals. This was where Mamá taught her class. This was where they told my mother they were sending her away to boarding school, and this was where my grandparents decided to end their forty-year marriage.

As I stepped off the cement slab and looked down, tears started rolling down my face. I felt a sadness that I had never felt before. It was old sadness. I was feeling Mamá's and my mother's pain, their loss. On the floor were old pieces of green tile that were part of the bathroom. I bent down and picked up a few pieces of the broken green tile and squeezed them in my hand, as if they were going to tell me what had happened to the house. Although the little green tiles didn't reveal what happened, they did speak to me. An inner voice said to me, "This is where you're from." I instantly felt a deep connection to this land. I was home.

Yes, I was born at the Jewish Memorial Hospital in Washington Heights, and I love New York and the United States, but that's not who I really am. With a name like Torres-Gongora and given my appearance, people always assume I'm not American, and ask me, "What are you? Where are you from?" What they really want to know is where was I born, and where does my family come from. I always give this lengthy explanation: I was born in Manhattan, my mother is Cuban, and my father is Puerto Rican. I had an epiphany while I was standing on the cement foundation of Santa Felicita with the broken tiles in my hand, in the middle of Cuba: *No one would ever ask me where I was from again. They would definitely know I was from here. They would know I was Cuban.*

I picked up a few more green tiles and put them in my pocket. I wanted to bring back a little piece of Santa Felicita.

The sun began to set, and we all got on the truck and started back to Las Tunas. On the way back, I felt that what I had just experienced was a dream. I couldn't believe that I had actually gone to Santa Felicita. Then I put my hands in my pockets and felt the little green tiles and knew it was real. When I got back to the United States, I gave the little green tiles to family members as souvenirs. By their appreciation and emotion, you would have thought I was giving them precious jewels. When I gave one to my mother, she squeezed it tight and began to cry.

"*Mi casa*," she said.

34

Camagüey

Me with cousins in Camagüey, Cuba.

We were all tired from the trip, but thank God my cousin Alicia stayed back and prepared dinner. Their dining room was the nicest room in the house. There was a long table with 12 chairs.

We all sat down to eat. Alicia brought out a platter and placed it on the table. It was the little black animal from the backyard. I never asked what kind of animal it was. She brought platters of white rice and sliced green tomatoes, too. The green tomatoes came from the countryside, about 15 miles out of town. My cousin Luis would ride his bicycle every morning to get the green tomatoes. We ate green tomatoes at every meal. I was very grateful for their efforts to have the best meals that their circumstances could provide. I knew they didn't normally eat this way, and they could get in trouble if they were found out by a *chivato*, a neighborhood government spy.

The food was very bland, not like the Cuban food I grew up with. It was because they didn't have any herbs and spices. Alicia said, "I did the best I could with one clove of garlic. I hope you like it."

"Of course," I told her. It was delicious, and I ate everything on my plate. I often think of my cousin Alicia when I'm cooking; making sofrito; or chopping up garlic, culantro, cilantro, onions, green peppers, cumin and oregano. I wish I could send her my sofrito so she could cook authentically. The Havana Club rum that I bought the day before from the hotel gift store made everything taste great. We all talked about what a wonderful day it was. How much we laughed, visiting our grandparents' ranch, Santa Felicita. I felt so fulfilled, so happy. I kept thinking, *I can't wait to tell my mother when I get back.*

But that still left Camagüey. I asked my cousin Eduardo, "Is there any way that we could go there?" Camagüey is the next province over, about two hours away.

He said, "There's this other guy in town who has a car and for a price, sometimes he drives people around."

"Can you ask him and see if he would take us?"

"Okay," he said. "Maybe tomorrow?"

Eduardo went to see the driver. Again, he came back with a big smile. "Yes, he will take you for $150."

"That's great."

"He'll pick you and Trudy up at 7 A.M."

I wondered if my old uncle Pancho would like to come. I went and asked him. He said yes. I said, "Meet us at 7 A.M., that's when the driver is coming."

"I'll be there."

Everything was going great. I got to see Santa Felicita, and now we were going to Camagüey.

The next morning, Trudy, Eduardo, and I got ready for our trip. Tío Pancho was at the door at 7 A.M. sharp. We all got in the car and headed to Camagüey. The roads were rough, but not as bad as the roads to Santa Felicita.

We arrived at this big Spanish colonial house. We knocked on the door of Tío Pancho's other granddaughter, Liliana, who opened the door. Again, tears rolled down my old uncle's face. This was his first time back in this house since the death of his only daughter, Alicia Elena. She had died five years earlier from a heart attack on New Year's Eve. She was only fifty years old.

My uncle made the introductions. My cousin Liliana lives with her husband, two children, and her father, Enrique. Enrique is the communist guy that my cousin Alicia Elena married. He played a big part in the revolution. He was the general in charge of Camagüey. He proudly took us right to his office. On the walls were lots of pictures of him with Castro and all kinds of certificates of honor. I thought, *This is wild. I'm actually seeing all this communist stuff.* Then Liliana took us to the courtyard. On the way there, we passed many rooms. Liliana stopped at one of the bedrooms, pointed to some beautiful antique furniture, and said, "That furniture belonged to your grandmother Alicia" (Mamá!). "She gave it to my mother before she left for the States."

The furniture was beautiful. In the United States, I'm sure this furniture would cost a small fortune. Naturally, I took photographs to show when I got back home. We sat in the courtyard drinking Cuban coffee. In the corner was this giant urn that they call a *tinajón*. This was used to collect rainwater in the old days. Camagüey is known as "La Tierra de los Tinajónes". This one had "1915" carved on its side. As I looked around, it was clear that these cousins were not struggling. They weren't poor like my cousins in Las Tunas. I'm sure their connection to the government had a lot to do with it.

That night, Liliana made dinner, and we sat in her formal dining room with lit candles on the table. Liliana's brother, Enriquito, came over with his kids. It became a big celebration. Enriquito asked Trudy and me if we wanted a mojito. I had never heard of a mojito before, but we said yes. It was a big production. He put sugar and fresh mint in a glass, and muddled them together until they were well blended. He then poured rum into the glass and stirred it with a thin piece of sugarcane. This was the most delicious drink I had ever tasted. Today, in the United States, mojitos are served everywhere.

I asked Enrique, the communist cousin, if he knew where my mother's house was, the one they lived in after leaving Santa Felicita. He said, "Of course. It's just a few blocks from here. Do you want to go see it?"

"I would really love that."

So we all started walking to the house where Mamá and mother had lived before they came to the United States. Before I left for Cuba, my mother had told me to knock on the neighbor's door, on the house to the left. She said they should still be there, if they were alive, because they never came to the United States. I loved seeing the townhouses placed next door to one another. They were like New York brownstones, except the architecture was Moorish, with carved wooden arched doors.

We got to my mother's house and knocked on the door. This very sweet lady answered. I said to her, "My mother lived here before she moved to the United States."

She said, "Come in, take a look around."

We all walked in. I started looking around. I wanted to take it all in: the marble columns, the porcelain tile with the Moorish design, the bright colored stained-glass windows, and the courtyard. The house was exactly as my mother described it. I was grateful that I was able to explore at least one of my mother's former homes.

As we were leaving, the nice lady handed me a miniature *tinajón* and said, "Give this to your mother and tell her this will always be her home. I'm just taking care of it for her."

I hugged her and thanked her. As we started to walk back to my cousin's house, I said to everyone, "Wait. I'm going to knock on the next-door neighbor's house to see if my mother's old neighbors still live here."

I knocked on the door, and I heard a woman's tiny voice asking *"Quien es?"*

She opened the door a little. She was less than five feet tall, with white hair and glasses as thick as Coke bottles.

I told her, "I'm Irma Gongora Peraza's son, from the family that lived next door in the nineteen-forties, before they moved to the United States."

She said, "Oh, *si*," gave me a smile, and started to close the door.

As she was closing the door, we heard a man's voice yelling, "*Espérate!*—wait!" It was her son, who opened the door and said, "You're Irma's son?"

"Yes."

"*Adelante!*—come on in! Sit down. How is your mother? We used to play cards together all the time. And how are . . ." He started asking about all my aunts and cousins, one by one. I brought him up to date.

He said, "You know, the sofa you are sitting on and all of our living-room furniture belonged to your grandmother. She was a great woman."

I asked him if he would mind if I took a picture of the furniture so I could show my mother. He said, "Not at all."

The furniture was in excellent condition. I guess they hardly sat in their living room. He was so excited to hear about his long-lost neighbors. We thanked him and went on our way.

The trip to Camagüey was a success. I had seen everything I wanted to see. We had to get back to Las Tunas, because our flight to Havana was scheduled for the next day.

35

Goodbye, My Cuban Family

LEFT: The *Playbill* for *Havana B.C.*, Coconut Grove Playhouse, 1995;
RIGHT: My sister Debbie and me, the night we won for the rumba at the 1973
Harvest Moon Ball, Madison Square Garden

We had one last party before we left. My cousin Alicia asked me, "Would you like to meet one of your grandfather's other sons? One of the three that he had with his mistress?"

I said, "Yes."

Apparently, he asked her to get permission from me first because he knew that my mother had never wanted to meet them. Even though my mother knew that her parents' breakup was not their fault, she still wanted nothing to do with them or anything that reminded her of the pain she felt at that time. Shortly after, Alicia invited my grandfather's only surviving son, Alvaro. He came in, and Alicia introduced us. He shook my hand, but his eyes never met mine. It was like he was almost ashamed of what had happened. I felt bad for him; after all, he was not responsible for my grandfather's choices.

In 1957, when my grandfather Miguel Angel died, my mother and my aunts went back to Cuba for his funeral. Castro was not yet in power. My grandfather's mistress and his three sons were there. My aunt Silvia had become friends with them. At the funeral, Tía Silvia asked my mother, "Do you want me to introduce you to your brothers?" My mother answered, "I have only two brothers, Miguel and Mario. I don't have any other brothers." She didn't realize that her half-brothers were standing right behind her when she said this. She felt bad, but she still would not agree to meet them. I'm glad I met Alvaro. He died shortly after I left Cuba.

It was time to pack our bags. I arranged for the guy who drove us to Camagüey to take us to the Holguín airport. When we arrived at the airport, they told us our flight was canceled, and the next flight to Havana was in three days. I said, "In three days! We will miss our flight to Miami," which was leaving in two days. What were Trudy and I going to do? We were a long way off, toward the other end of Cuba.

The driver then said, "I'll drive you to Havana for $200."

We said, "Great! Let's go."

"Okay, I'll pick you up in a couple of hours. It takes about ten hours to get to Havana from here."

My cousins and I hugged and kissed with watery eyes. We knew we might never see each other again. In those couple of days, my cousins and I grew to love each other as if we had known each other all our lives. Trudy and I left my cousins everything we could. This was a trip of a lifetime. I will always be grateful to my Cuban cousins. My heart was so full.

It was time to go. We got in the car and kept waving until we couldn't see each other anymore. Thank God the driver knew all the places to get gas along the way, because getting gas in Cuba at that time was not easy. Fortunately, the flight cancellation enabled Trudy and me to see almost the entire island. The driver got us back to Havana on time, and we caught our flight home.

When I got off the plane in Miami, I couldn't believe I had been to Cuba. I was walking on air. I ran to the first payphone and called my mother. "Mom, I'm back. Cuba was amazing. I'll tell you all about it when I see you." When I told my mother of all the places I'd seen, it was bittersweet. She was happy that I had experienced her childhood places but sad about how it all had changed.

As soon as Trudy and I got back to Provincetown, we returned to our plan to have a baby. Sadly, however, despite several visits to a fertility doctor for the necessary procedures, our goal was not realized. Naturally disappointed, Trudy adopted a beautiful newborn boy from San Antonio, Texas. She named her son Jesse Miguel. She used Miguel in honor of my maternal grandfather, and because she loved the name. Trudy has done an incredible job raising Jesse. He is now almost twenty-five years old and a college graduate. Trudy and I remain best friends, and Jesse and I have a loving, close relationship. It's one kind of modern family. Every once in a while, Trudy and I go through the pictures we took while were in Cuba and say to each other, "Wasn't it great that we got to visit Cuba when we did." Many of the pictures we took were of the places Mamá and my mother told me about. I no longer have to envision these places. The Palm trees, Santa Felicita, my grandmother's house—I was there. I was in Cuba.

One year later, inspired by my trip to Cuba's Tropicana nightclub, as well as by various Cuban artists and memories of my parents, I wrote a show called *Havana B.C.* (Havana before Castro). The show, about Havana's heyday, paid homage to Cuban and American composers, singers, and dances of that time. Many of the Cuban numbers were by composer Ernesto Lecuona. Tributes included Nat King Cole (who sang in Spanish with his charming American accent), Desi Arnaz, and Andy Russell to name a few. I sang all of the songs we think of as American standards that are actually Latin American standards, singing both English and Spanish versions. The dances I performed along with my dance partner and sister, Debbie, included the rumba, cha cha, tango, samba, conga, and of course, the mambo. Incidentally, we were the rumba champions at the 1973 Harvest Moon Ball, which was held in Madison Square Garden.

Havana B.C. previewed in New York at Don't Tell Mama, with musical direction by Alex Rybeck and direction by Sara Louise Lazarus. After two years of sold-out performances and winning *Backstage*'s Bistro Award for best theme, *Havana B.C.* was "hijacked" to Florida's Coconut Grove Playhouse. The run was a dream come true; a three-month success. The last number of the show was *Siempre en Mi Corazón (Always in My Heart)*. I introduced this song with the words, "A wall came down in Berlin, now it's time for the wall to come down in Cuba."

36

Finding My Roots

The Peraza
Family Crest

During one of my afternoon conversations with Mamá, she told me, matter-of-factly, that our ancestors, the Perazas, had been king and queen of the Canary Islands. Unfortunately, we were interrupted, and the discussion never went further. I know some Cubans tend to exaggerate, but I knew Mamá would never make up such a fantastic story. That same day I asked my mother if she knew that our ancestors were royalty of the Canary Islands. She said "Yes, I heard that, but that's all I know." I was totally fascinated, but time slipped away, and I never got to hear more of the story directly from Mamá. Many years passed before I decided to do my own research. I'm a huge fan of ancestry programs like *Who Do You Think You Are?* and *Finding Your Roots*. And I have always been curious to find out who my ancestors were.

I began my search with Ancestry (www.ancestry.com) and by reading every Spanish history book about discoverers, conquerors, and royalty of the Canary Islands. On the Ancestry website I connected my roots up to my great-grandfather Florencio's (Mama's father's) generation, but that's as far as I got. Through Ancestry, I started receiving emails from cousins I had never met before. The e-mails came from Cuba, Spain, and Florida, asking me questions about my family's ancestry. I knew a lot of the answers to their questions, since Mamá was the oldest of her siblings and shared so many stories with me, but I couldn't confirm the Canary Islands royalty connection.

Not being very successful in my search, I put it on hold. Then, out of the blue, I received an e-mail from a woman named Mirelis Peraza. In her e-mail, she told me that she had been working on the Peraza family tree for years, and had several connecting branches that go back very far. Getting this email from Mirelis was life changing. We immediately exchanged phone numbers, and the airwaves began to burn. Mirelis was also born in Sagua la Grande, Cuba, the same town where Mamá was born and where her family still lives.

Comparing our stories, it was clear we must be related. We both had heard that we had descended from the king and queen of the Canary Islands, and that one of our ancestors was General Peraza who fought in the Spanish-American War and helped liberate Cuba. Although Mirelis had completed a lot of the research on the Peraza branches, she was unable to connect her family to Canary Island royalty. Mirelis asked me for my grandparents' and great-grandparents' names, including the maiden names, to see if one of the branches that she had completed was mine. In Cuba, women never drop their maiden names. After a woman is married, she just adds her husband's name to all of her own. For example, my mother's name was Irma Gloria Andrea de la Caridad Peraza Gongora. When she married my father, her name became Irma Gloria Andrea de la Caridad Peraza Gongora de

Torres. In the United States, she gave her name simply as Irma Gloria Torres.

I remembered my mother telling me that as a child, she was taught to recite all of her ancestors' last names going back four generations. At this time, my mother was eighty-five years old and was suffering from dementia. As she would say, "My back memory is perfect, but I can't tell you what day it is." I called her immediately to see if she could still recite her ancestors' last names.

I asked her, "Do you still remember all your past last names?"

Sure enough, she rattled off every last name, just as she did when she was a little girl. I called Mirelis immediately with the names. She said, "I have good news for you! I have your line connected to the first Perazas who came to Cuba, and who were direct descendants of the Canary Islands' royal family."

With this amazing news. I filled in all the names in my genealogical tree. I also verified each name through the Spanish Ancestry site. But I wanted to know more than just their names, so I continued to read every book that referenced the Perazas.

The first-known record of the Peraza family is in Seville, Spain, dating back to the 1300s. It felt surreal, reading my family name in these history books. The House of Peraza was among the Spanish nobility that explored and conquered the Canary Islands. This was so exciting that I couldn't stop reading. These people were no longer characters in a history book; these were actually my ancestors. I kept reading. Now I wanted to know what happened to them.

The Perazas first came to the Canary Islands during the 1300s, but they didn't settle there until the late 1400s. Adding to the other titles they already held, they were recognized by the court of Spain as the royal family of the seven main islands. Early on, however, they faced many uprisings of the indigenous peoples, who were called Guanches and Gomeros. During one of the first uprisings, one of the Gomeros hit King Hernán Peraza the Elder with a stone, killing him instantly. Upon his death, his sister, Inez Peraza de las Casas, my eleventh great-grandmother, became Queen of the Canary Islands. When I first read about this, I felt bad for Hernán. On the other hand, I knew that Spanish conquistadors weren't the nicest people. The Gomeros were only defending what was theirs.

In the early 1400s, the seven Canary Islands had been divided into *menceyatos*, or small kingdoms. Hernán Peraza the Younger, Ines's son, my tenth great-grandfather, with the title El Conde (Count), initially ruled the islands La Gomera and El Hierro. He then became king of all seven islands. His queen, my tenth great-grandmother, was Beatriz de Bobadilla y Ossorio, also known as Beatriz la Cazadora "Beatriz the Huntress"

This ancestor of mine was a lady-in-waiting to Spain's Queen Isabella, and her aunt—with almost the same name, Beatriz de Bobadilla—was Queen Isabella's childhood friend and adviser. My ancestor was also a lover to King Ferdinand. Upon learning about the affair, Queen Isabella gave her an ultimatum: "Lose your head, or leave the Royal Household forever." The only reason she was given any choice at all was because she was the niece of the queen's best friend. It was King Ferdinand who arranged for her to marry Hernán Peraza the Younger. Obviously, she agreed.

Soon after Beatriz's arrival in the Canaries and marriage to Hernán Peraza the Younger, Queen Isabella and King Ferdinand demoted them from King and Queen of the Canary Islands to Duke and Duchess of the islands La Gomera and El Hierro and also gave them a handsome sum of money as a consolation. Their demotion did not stop the Gomeros from defending their land and continue fighting with the Spanish conquerors. A few years later, Hernán Peraza the Younger was killed with a dart by the local Gomeros after being caught red-handed having an affair with their leader's fiancée. This event provoked the Gomeros to attack the Spaniards even more. Beatriz along with her children barricaded themselves in the Torre del Conde until Queen Isabella sent Pedro de Vera, governor of Gran Canaria, the third largest of the Canary Islands, to free and defend her.

Pedro de Vera was ruthless. He ordered the deaths of all males over the age of fifteen by decapitation, hanging, or drowning. Some of the woman were sent to slavery. This was the last uprising; Beatriz now became the ruler. Beatriz was as ruthless as she was beautiful. In revenge for the assassination of her husband and for the protection of her family, she executed many of the remaining Gomeros. Beatriz, now ruler of La Gomera and El Hierro, was very wealthy and decided to invest in sugarcane plantations. All the Peraza generations that followed prospered from the sugar plantations until the Caribbean islands became the center of the sugar trade. I had mixed feelings about what I had read about my ancestors.

On Christopher Columbus's famous voyage, he stopped at the Canary Islands on his way to the New World to replenish his three ships. Beatriz and Columbus had a love affair during his stay. Mesmerized by her, he changed his original plan, which was to stay for a couple of days. Instead, he stayed for over a month. Before Columbus sailed, Beatriz gave him lots of supplies. A year later, on his second voyage, he met her again, and among her gifts this time were sugarcane clippings. That's how sugarcane first came to the Caribbean. Although the initial attempts at cultivation faltered, eventually the crop was the basis for my great grandfather's plantation. In 1498, on his third voyage, Columbus returned to the Canary Islands and found Beatriz married to Pedro Fernández de Lugo, another conquistador.

Ironically, the sugar business declined in the Canary Islands when the Caribbean sugar industry prospered. This led the Peraza descendants to emigrate to Cuba. In the 1760s, four Peraza brothers went to four different Cuban provinces, began their sugar plantations, and became very successful. The plantation in Sagua la Grande was passed directly from generation to generation all the way to Mamá's father Florencio, my great-grandfather—the big man in the oval picture that hung in Mamá's Nagle Avenue living room wall. This was amazing. Everything Mamá had told me was true.

My mother always said I was a "Peraza." I asked her, "What does this mean?" She said that I was like her mother's side of the family.

I asked my mother, "In what way am I a Peraza?"

She said, *"Los Perazas son muy orgullosos*—The Perazas are very proud."

I said, "I'm not a snob."

My mother then said, "No, but you like the finer things in life, and you are very artistic. You are very much like Mamá."

I often wonder why I am so interested in my family history. Something in me is always digging into who and what part of me comes from my ancestors. I wonder what traits I carry in my DNA. The older I get, the more I become like my parents. I'm sure that many people feel that way. As my mother got older, she took on more of Mamá's looks and mannerisms. I feel comfort in immersing myself in the traditions of all the people who came before me, especially what I inherited from Mamá. If you don't know where you came from, how are you to know who you really are?

37

Perazas at La Gomera

LEFT: The Torre del Conde, La Gomera, the Canary Islands;
RIGHT: A painting of my tenth great-grandmother Beatriz de Bobadilla y Ossorio

In 2014, after learning about my ancestors' history, I decided to visit the places they had come from. My first stop was Seville, Spain. I had been in Seville in 2003 with my mother. I remember her saying, "I love Seville. I feel very at home here. I love the music, the flamenco dancing, and the dresses." At the time we had no idea we were in a town where our ancestors had lived.

With all my gathered information, I started my investigation. I walked all over town, searching from building to building until finally,

I ended up at the right place. I walked into what seemed like a museum. I was told to go to the second floor. I walked into an office with these women all dressed in white doctor's coats and white gloves. They looked like they were getting ready to perform an operation. Their faces were stern and expressionless. They were scary.

I told them that I was looking for information about my ancestors. They handed me three reference books, and sent me to a table to do my research. I came across several references to the Peraza name. I went back to the ladies in white and asked for the books. They strictly told me that I could take one book out at a time. That was understandable. In one book, it said that a Peraza had been one of the twenty-four founding fathers of Seville. I asked if I could make a copy of my findings. In a very blunt manner, they said, "No, and you cannot take any pictures, nor take notes."

I spent the rest of that day and the next two days trying to absorb as much as I could read. I verified all of what I had read in the history books.

The next day, I flew to Gran Canaria, the third largest of the seven main Canary Islands. I took a bus down the east coast to Puerto de Mogan. Through Airbnb, I rented a charming little room by the ocean. The room was in a hostel on the side of the mountain. The hostel was painted in a psychedelic style, and had crazy tile work. I thought I was back in the sixties. A pretty young woman showed me to my room, and said that this was the best room in the house. Indeed, it was beautiful. It faced the ocean and had a private balcony that came with a cat. Every night, all the guests would gather in the main room with guitars and beer. I stayed up with them until the wee hours, singing songs.

After three days, it was time for me to go to La Gomera, the island my ancestors came from. A woman from the hostel offered me a ride to the bus that would take me to the ferry for Tenerife, the largest island.

The bus ride to the ferry was the scariest ride of my life. We rode through the highest mountain on winding, single-lane roads without guardrails. It was as steep as the Empire State Building. I closed my eyes and started praying. With my eyes closed, I could hear these two women talking about everyday stuff, without a care in the world. I asked them, "Aren't you afraid we're going to die?"

They laughed and kept on talking.

I made it to the ferry with just five minutes to spare, and was off to Tenerife. It was cloudy with an occasional sprinkle. When I arrived, a bus was waiting to take us to the ferry to La Gomera. La Gomera is the second smallest and of the main Canary Islands. I boarded the ferry and went outside on the front deck, waiting to spot the island. The sun was now shining bright, without a cloud in sight, and the wind was blowing in my face.

We pulled into a small harbor that was right in the center of the town. I got into a cab and gave the driver the address of my Airbnb rental. He drove about three blocks and made a U-turn, and there I was. It would have been quicker to walk.

The Airbnb host opened the door to a beautiful courtyard full of plants. His wife came down with a banana smoothie and handed it to me. It was so delicious. We exchanged small talk while they showed me to my room, which was gorgeous, with a private bath and entrance. They asked me, "What brings you to La Gomera?"

I told them, "I'm a Peraza, a descendant of the Perazas of La Gomera."

"*Dios mío*, my hairs are all standing on end. Right at the center of town, there is a park with a medieval tower, the Torre del Conde, remaining from the Perazas' reign. You could walk there; it's only five minutes away."

I thanked them, put my bag down, and off I went.

I went down this narrow cobblestone street to the end and made a right turn, and there was the park with my ancestors' tower. It wasn't as big as I imagined. It stands about fifty feet high, but it's the most important monument of La Gomera. It had a plaque with the Peraza name on it. I felt like I had actually traveled back in time.

I put my hand on it, feeling the vibrations of my ancestors. I closed my eyes and said, "I'm here, Mamá. You were right. We come from the king and queen of the Canary Islands."

I continued walking through the narrow, small-town streets. I stopped at a bakery and bought some local delicacies. There were many little cafes with tapas. I tasted as many as I could.

As I was walking back to the house, I passed a tour group in front of this little museum. I decided to go inside the museum. There were many old portraits. I went around looking at them. I came to a portrait of a beautiful woman: it was Beatriz de Bobadilla—Beatrice the Beauty—my tenth great-grandmother. I couldn't hold back my excitement. I told the museum guard that she was my ancestor. He shook my hand with a big smile and welcomed me to La Gomera. My journey searching for my ancestors came to a satisfying end.

After three days I arranged for a cab to take me to the airport. I said goodbye to my wonderful hosts, and off I went.

On the way to the airport, the driver said, "You're a Peraza."

"Yes, how did you know?"

"Everyone in town has heard a Peraza was here."

All I could think of was Mamá. I wished she were still alive so that I could tell her about my trip and everything I had learned about the Perazas.

Mamá was the greatest influence of my life.

Epilogue

Every once in a while, I gaze at Mamá's paintings and imagine her in Cuba at the back of her house, wearing her *pamela* and holding the paintbrushes she made from her horse's tail. This was when her young heart was full of hopes and dreams of spending the rest of her life with her beloved Miguel Angel. Although life did not turn out the way she thought it would, Mamá was able to pass on her dignity, strength, and most of all, the love of family to all of us.

My mother was right. I am like Mamá, a true Peraza. Like her I love to paint, write, and sing. And yes, I appreciate the finer things in life.

Epilogue

About the Author

Born and raised in New York City, Ron Torres graduated with a BFA in music from The City University of New York (The Leonard Davis Center for The Performing Arts). A talented singer, actor, and ballroom dancer, he has appeared in many of the city's top cabarets, and won a *Backstage* Bistro Award, "Best Theme," for his show *Havana B.C.* He has also performed in several operas at the Met and with the Florida Grand Opera. He and his sister Debbie took top honors for the rumba at the 1973 Harvest Moon Ball held in Madison Square Garden. His theater credits include over twenty productions, regionally and in New York City. An accomplished painter as well, he has exhibited his artwork in galleries in Provincetown and New York City. This is Ron's first time out as a writer, and he foresees more writing projects to follow.